A fascinating book about one of seaside towns. Although I have bee times it's amazing how much I d place and its history and how unol when walking around!

The walks are all short and easily manageable and keep you informed at all times. The locals seem to know about the book and it gained me access to the Purbeck Hotel to look around the historic rooms and gardens. It's written in an easy to read style and I found that I had almost read it all on the day I got it. If you love Swanage you'll love this book, but even if you are a first-time visitor it means you will get so much more from your visit.

(Amazon reviewer)

This book tells the story through all the people that make Swanage such a friendly, welcoming place: we actually meet the volunteer lifeboatmen and Coastwatch teams, the incredible people who restored and now run the local steam railway, the local fishermen and – unusually – all the enterprising, ingenious, creative people who produce special Purbeck produce. This is not at the expense of the main points of interest ...

Exploring all the town's interesting features forms a substantial section of the book. Simple, clear maps, good use of colour to highlight questions and beautiful photography identifying features make it easy to use on the move.

(Jean Sutton, author and retired publisher)

I think it is the most interesting book about the town that I have read.

(Lin Dorey, Swanage resident, www.virtual-swanage.co.uk)

Lesser Known
Swanage

Julie Musk

Roving
Press

© 2009, 2014 by Julie Musk

Published by Roving Press Ltd
4 Southover Cottages, Frampton, Dorset, DT2 9NQ, UK
Tel: +44 (0)1300 321531
www.rovingpress.co.uk

First published 2009 by Roving Press Ltd
Second revised edition 2014.

ISBN: 978-1-906651-03-9

British Library Cataloguing in Publication Data
A catalogue record for this book is available from the British Library

Photographs and maps by Roving Press unless stated otherwise.
Cover design by Tim Musk using photographs by Simon Twilley, David Leadbetter, Dom Greves and Angela Bird.
Frontispiece photograph by Simon Twilley

Set in 11.5/13 pt by Beamreach Printing (www.beamreachuk.co.uk)
Printed and bound in England by Henry Ling Ltd., at the Dorset Press, Dorchester, DT1 1HD.

Contents

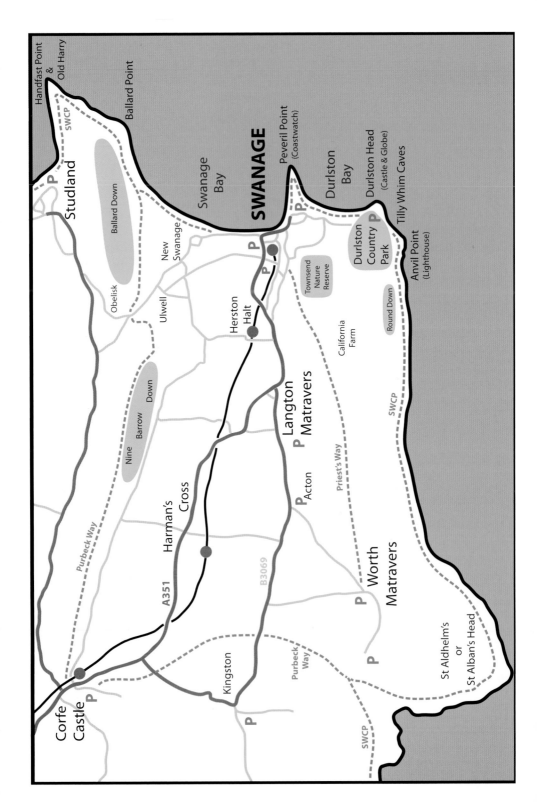

Foreword

I welcome this opportunity to provide a few words of introduction to Julie Musk's *Lesser Known Swanage.* Here is a new book that provides a fresh view of Swanage. Interesting topics of local history are complemented by a series of walks and quiz questions, which will enable residents and visitors to explore this unique town, and discover numerous fascinating features that include many old London relics. A vivid picture of Swanage today is given through interviews with local people involved in many different occupations and leisure activities, ranging from bee-keeping and cheese making to sea rowing and rock climbing.

Concise sections on quarrying and the stone trade, the development of Swanage as a tourist resort, and the principal characters in its development, John Mowlem and George Burt, provide the historical background to why Swanage came to look the way it does today. Julie's imaginative approach to describing historical figures and landmarks, such as George Burt and the Wellington Clock Tower, will undoubtedly appeal to a younger audience.

Although I have always been a resident of Swanage, and have researched many aspects of the town's history, I found out about all sorts of new 'lesser known' facts by reading this book. Everything from what happened to the wheel from an old stone cart at Purbeck House to geocaching – what is that about you may say? – if you read this book you will find out!

The sections on Regular Events and Local Fare and Produce will give a flavour – no pun intended – of what Swanage has to offer to locals and visitors throughout the year. The book concludes with useful sections on sources of information, such as the library and museum, together with a list of books for further reading.

This is a handy book that I recommend to you as one not only to add to your bookshelf, but also to take out and discover Swanage, both past and present.

David Haysom
Hon. Curator
Swanage Museum

Preface

Lesser Known Swanage is the first in a series of *Lesser Known Guides* we are publishing under Roving Press. Marcel Proust (French novelist) commented, 'The real voyage of discovery consists not in seeking new landscapes but in having new eyes'. This encapsulates what the *Guides* set out to do. Rather like having your own local guide to show you around, to give you a different perspective, *Lesser Known Swanage* aims to bring Swanage places and people alive, to provide a snapshot of real life – past and present. I hope it also encourages you to revisit favourite haunts, to see them in a new light. Moreover, it aims to support local people, businesses and organisations, highlighting what is on offer to locals and visitors alike.

Stories and reminiscences are usually more memorable than facts, and this book hopes, above all, to be a good story. I met and talked to so many interesting local people, all of whom generously provided an insight into their lives; others I'm sure would have just as absorbing experiences to tell, but unfortunately I had to call a halt somewhere. The story of Swanage is very much their story – their narrative makes up a large part of the book, interspersed with factual details and my personal observations.

With two young children, I know how hard it is to spark and maintain interest, so this book is written with families and young people in mind, sometimes using an imaginative style that should appeal to younger readers. As you take the book out and follow the walks, they can look for clues and answers to the quiz questions, perhaps allowing you some breathing space.

Julie Musk

Acknowledgements

Thanks to everyone who contributed or helped with the book, in any way. In particular, Bob Campbell, Chris Caruana, Barry and Phyl England, Trev Haysom, Martin Payne, Ross Prior, Chris Suttle, Ali Tuckey, Dave and Malcolm Turnbull, Andrew Wright, and the Lifeboat and Coastwatch crews.

Special thanks to David Haysom for checking and in most cases supplying the historical information, and leading me on many a walk around his home town.

Also thanks to Peter John Cooper (www.spyway.co.uk) for the poems, taken from his performance poetry stage show Field of Fantasy.

A number of people kindly supplied photographs and are credited in the captions. Particular thanks go to Chris and Simon Twilley.

Remember
SWANAGE

PEOPLE USUALLY DO

For further information and a free copy of the Town Guide
please write to: Dept. BR Tourist Office, Swanage. Dorset BH19 1LB
or telephone Swanage (0929) 422885.

Introduction

'We're going southwest for the hols,' says Faith.
'If only it was Swanage again!'

(Enid Blyton,
Adventure of the Strange Ruby, p.13)

Swanage still has that old-fashioned charm that Enid Blyton wrote about, giving it a different feel to neighbouring seaside places. Moreover it regularly boasts more sunshine hours than any other British resort.

Swanage was little more than a fishing village and stone port until the early 1800s, when William Morton Pitt, M.P. for Dorset, began developing it as a resort:

> *'... impressed with the beauty of the situation of Swanwich and the salubrity of its climate, and finding the shore of smooth fine sand to be admirably adapted for sea bathing, (W.M.P.) first conceived the idea of raising it to the condition of a watering place'.*

Huge amounts of land were up for sale and Pitt bought the whole quay area. He built the stone quay, Preventive Station and Marine Villa on the Pier, which offered coffee rooms, a billiard room and salt-water baths (which are still under the floor today) so bathers could enjoy the water without having to brave the open sea. He also built a customs house and library. However, it was slow going as the only real access to the town at that time was by sea; he must have bitten off more than he could chew as he ended up bankrupt, though did manage to keep the *small* family dwelling of Kingston Maurward House, near Dorchester.

Another name very much associated with Swanage is George Burt, nephew of John Mowlem, founder of the great building firm Mowlem. Burt brought the railway, gas, fresh water and a drainage system to Swanage. He is also responsible for the town's nickname 'Old London by the Sea' – Burt was an original recycler and collector of junked decorative pieces from London building sites at the time, bringing them back to Swanage in his stone boats as ballast and adorning his home town with them. It is he we should thank for the many interesting and quirky features that are found in Swanage today.

Thomas Hardy wrote most of his novel *The Hand of Ethelberta* (1876) while lodging at the house of a former sea captain in Swanage. He came to know the small village (as it then was) intimately, calling it Knollsea in his stories:

> *'Knollsea had recently begun to attract notice in the world. It had this year undergone visitation from a score of professional gentlemen and their wives, a minor canon, three marine painters, seven young ladies with books in their hands, and nine-and-thirty babies. Hence a few lodging-houses, of a dash and pretentiousness far beyond the mark of the old cottages which formed the original substance of the village, had been erected to meet the wants of such as these.'*

To Thomas and Emma Hardy, honeymooning in Swanage, the cliffs and headlands of Purbeck were similar to the Cornwall of their courtship, and obviously fired Hardy's imagination, as he also wrote at least six poems inspired by the area. However, until the coming of the railway in 1885, the Isle of Purbeck was quite isolated. Consequently the inhabitants of Swanage were rather cut off from the world.

> *'The knowledge of the inhabitants was of the same special sort as their pursuits. The quarrymen in white fustian understood practical geology, the laws and accidents of dips, faults, and cleavage, far better than the ways of the world and mammon; the seafaring men in Guernsey frocks had a clearer notion of Alexandria, Constantinople, the Cape, and the Indies than of any inland town in their own country. This, for them, consisted of a busy portion, the Channel, where they lived and laboured, and a dull portion, the vague unexplored miles of interior at the back of the ports, which they seldom thought of.'*
>
> (Thomas Hardy, *The Hand of Ethelberta*)

Development of the area continued slowly. There was talk of building a breakwater to create a port to make the Bay useful for shipping, but this was decried in favour of keeping Swanage superior and apart. The Navy was barred 'because sailors talk loudly, drink a little beer, and are disturbing to the selectness of a place' (Benfield, 1990, p.21). The town essentially attracted the middle classes, and still does.

Stewart Borrett interviewed local people who grew up in Swanage in the 1920s and 1930s; below is an extract from his book, which describes the town's uniqueness:

> *'Unlike so many places then, that went through such grinding poverty, Swanage fared better than most. As close as north Somerset there were starvation marches held by the unemployed throughout the thirties, and*

yet there was nothing like that here. Why? Certainly the fact that the town was a holiday resort helped it through this period. The strong connection with London that started in Victorian times, with John Mowlem and George Burt, continued through the 1920s and 1930s with the two or three week holiday by the seaside being taken very seriously. As Norah Kaye said, "everyone did apartments" and many Swanage folk even moved out of their homes to let their houses to the holidaymakers. As well as the tourist industry, quarrying provided many jobs, as did the building industry, which thrived at the time with five building firms in the town. The retail trade probably employed the most people, though wages were low.'

(Borrett, 2002)

Swanage only really became popular with holidaymakers in the 20th century, and Enid Blyton helped to popularise it when she made it the model for Toy Town. So, in the 21st century, what has Swanage got to offer visitors? What hidden gems may even locals find surprising and inspiring? This book hopes to give you a real sense of place and time. As you begin to appreciate the history that has gone into building Swanage, the people and industry involved, you will see there is more to the town than a fine sandy beach and the obvious tourist attractions.

What 'hidden gems' has Swanage got to offer?

An Observation

Poet and playwright Peter John Cooper used to live in Swanage and makes some interesting observations:

> 'Not only are the buildings made up of layers, so is our society. There's a social strata. People have certain stations – the lifeboatmen, the coastguards, the fire brigade, the fishermen, the sea rowers. Also there are lots of volunteer amateur organisations in the town – indicative of people having the time – a lot of us don't have proper jobs, are self-employed or retired. My dentist once had to disappear mid-op to man the lifeboat. There's a certain cache to belonging to a group or volunteer organisation; it earns you Brownie points. Your 'tribe' is defined by which volunteer organisation you belong to, be it your church, an art group or a particular sport. People who get paid to do something are slightly frowned upon – we are amateurs in the best and worst sense of the word! The scouts and guides here are like the mafia – you feel very proud to be invited into their organisation, and they raise zillions of pounds. It's the same with the carnival committee. In Swanage, compared to elsewhere, you are less defined by your job. This is what helps knit our community. But the downside is that people can become a bit cliquey and you need to belong and conform to certain groups to get on. I guess I'm part of the gossipy, arty, left-bank, café group. There's also a big pub culture – which impinges on young people. As soon as they reach 18 they must choose which pub to frequent.
> That's why it takes 20 years or so to become part of Swanage.'

Peter lived in Swanage for 20 years but still regarded himself as a newcomer and outsider. This attitude is apparent with other locals, one shopkeeper commenting he had *only* lived here for 30 years.

The Stone Trade

Purbeck stone is the cause of much local pride, and rightly so. Its quarrying goes back at least to AD 43, when the Romans invaded Britain; recognising its hardness and beauty they used the limestone for tombstones, memorials and other grand architecture.

Purbeck marble is not a true marble but a limestone, made up of the small shells of freshwater snails, that can be polished. The greyish-green seams top the Purbeck Beds. The marble needs skillful working as it is very hard. You can see fine examples in Salisbury Cathedral and more locally in the font of St Mary's Church, Swanage. During the Middle Ages they used it for coffin lids, fonts, effigies and monuments, both in England and abroad. Many of the quarry-owners and marblers lived at nearby Corfe, where they worked on the raw material before it was dispatched as finished stone all over the country. In the late Middle Ages, tastes changed and Purbeck marble went out of fashion as alabaster became more easily attainable. However, it was still popular up to the 16th century for tombs.

After the Reformation, church demand understandably petered out, but Purbeck stone continued to be quarried for secular buildings, including many Dorset manor houses, roofing and paving. Then following the Great Fire of London in 1666, there was a huge increase in demand for rebuilding. Kerbstones and foot pavements did not come in until the 1760s Paving Acts; Duke Street in London is said to have been the first to have had the convenience of a pavement – made of Purbeck stone. Gradually other old cobbled footways were abandoned and laid with flagstones and kerbing. Daniel Defoe, speaking of Purbeck in 1724, said:

> '*This part of the country is eminent for vast quarries of stone which is cut out flat and used in London … It is very profitable to the place, as also is the number of shipping employed in bringing it to London.*'

By the end of the 18th century/beginning of the 19th, thousands of tons of stone were being shipped from Swanage each year. The stone trade was at its height, and Purbeck marble can be found in many of our great old cathedrals.

John Mowlem and George Burt – Principal Characters in Swanage's Development

There are two principal characters in the history of Swanage, and both were stone masons. John Mowlem was born in Swanage in 1788. In true Dick Whittington style, he started out as a poor quarry boy, then left to seek his fortune in London as a stone mason, but it was Guernsey granite as well as Purbeck stone that would ultimately make him wealthy. He soon founded the great contracting firm Mowlem, employing his nephew, George Burt, who later became his partner. Through ambition, hard work and sheer good timing, the two made their fortunes in London through stone. John died in 1868, having retired to his native town a happy and rich man, and George succeeded him in the business. Both men enthusiastically left their mark on Swanage – improving the ancient high street, building more roads, the railway, the Mowlem Institute and Town Hall, and installing piped water, among other noteworthy achievements.

A Little Lesson in Geology

The Wessex Vales are made up of layers of limestone, sand and clay; these were laid down during Jurassic times when sea levels were changing. In the Cretaceous period, the layers were overlain by marine sediments (chalk and Upper Greensand), which have eroded away, exposing the Jurassic rocks

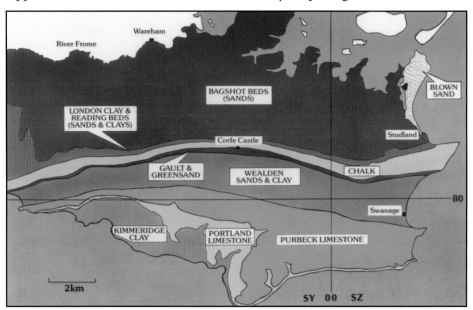

A simple geology of the Isle of Purbeck. (Courtesy of David Kemp and Leeson House Field Studies Centre.)

beneath. Folding and faulting resulted in some of these chalk layers being pushed up into near-vertical beds. Conversely, the limestone layers inland have remained comparatively flat, making them easy to dig out. Down through the centuries, these rocks have been quarried – the limestone used for buildings, roads and as lime, the sands for mortar, and the clays for bricks (see 'Swanage Brickworks', below).

Purbeck stone is made up of over 70 different beds, the different colours producing an attractive patterned variation in stone buildings, walls and paving. The stone is sedimentary Cretaceous/Upper Jurassic limestone and its low clay content makes it very hard.

A Honeycombed Landscape

Stone was quarried in the open where possible and from small underground 'quarrs' employing only four or so men. Up until World War II, most were family-run, and the last underground shaft was sunk in the 1950s. The coastal fields around Swanage are riddled with the remains of these small quarrs, with some shafts reaching down 36 m (120 ft).

Men worked along the line of a vein of stone, leaving one bed as a ceiling, which was propped up with supports. Levering out the clay between the limestone beds, a block of stone could then be removed. The men often worked in lanes only a metre high. They loaded their flat-bed cart with stone, which was then brought to the surface by pony or donkey power. The donkey was hitched to a long wooden arm, attached to a capstan, and by walking round in a circle would haul the stone up out of the quarry. Quarrymen worked in the open-sided sheds around the quarr, cutting and shaping the rough stone. The cut stone was then sent down to the town for storing at the 'bankers' or was shipped directly.

An old quarry at Durlston.

Cliff Quarrying

Along the cliffs, quarrymen cut galleries horizontally into the cliffs, then extracted blocks of stone along the bedding planes and joints. A jib was used to lower the stone into small boats waiting off the rocks. The crew of (usually) two in their sturdy rowing boats could carry up to 9 tons of stone at a time.

> 'When the boat was fully laden, the tough loaders would row back to the waiting vessels with little free board on their craft …they would only need to ship a couple of waves and the dead weight boat would sink quickly to the bottom beneath the crew … causing cheers and laughter from the shore based quarrymen'. (Ashley 1992)

Tilly Whim Caves at Durlston is one example of a cliff quarry, worked around 1700 to 1820. Evidence of gunpowder has been found in the caves. During the Napoleonic Wars, stone was in great demand for south-coast fortifications. After the War, demand slumped and the caves saw more activity from smugglers as a temporary store for contraband. In 1887 the Caves opened as a tourist attraction, but closed in 1976 following a rock fall. Today, bats and nesting birds are the only visitors.

Moving the Stone

Stone was either cut and shaped on site by quarrymen, many of whom were skilled stone masons, or brought down to town from the inland quarries by horse and cart. It was then stacked all along the shore, from beyond the Brook to the stone quay – an area known as the 'bankers' – and this area was used for storing and working stone for almost 200 years. Incidentally, the earlier stone quay was built by the parish, the quarriers supplying the stone and a day's work each.

Imagine the scene: heaps of stone lining the shore; men loading the rough-hewn blocks into the back of special high-wheeled carts (the wheels up to 6 ft in diameter) in the water; the stomp and tail flicking of the horses as they are goaded into action and wade out into the deeper water; a couple of loaders in each small rowing boat holding steady to receive the stone; the horses now up to their chests in the water; waves bouncing the little boats up and down as the men man-handle the stone off the back of the carts into their boats; their strong arms taking to the oars as they row their cargo out to the waiting ketches in the bay; a second crew lean over the side to raise the heavy stone by hand or derrick and bring it up onto the deck of the larger vessel; sails flapping, the captain declares the ship laden and ready to set sail; the stone is off.

The whole process was very labour intensive and dangerous. Thomas Hardy sketched the men laboriously unloading stone from the horse-drawn carts among the waves. You can see his small pencil drawing from his diary in the Dorset County Museum.

Loading stone in the Bay. Divers have found stacks of stone where it was inadvertently dropped in the sea. (From the David Haysom collection.)

In an effort to streamline the process, a wooden pier was built in 1859 with plans to lay a track 3 miles inland to the quarries at Langton. Trucks of stone could be pulled by horses on the narrow gauge to the new pier or pushed by hand. Henry Gillingham Jr, a stone merchant, was all for it:

> *'No longer must the din of the incessant mallet, from earliest dawn until evening, annoy the ears of invalids, nor the heavy shower of chips and scars flying around far and wide, endanger the lives of passengers by alarming horses unused to such salutations, to say nothing of blocks of stone invading the highways, or huge and unwieldy loading carts barring farther progress.'*

However, the system proved unpopular due to the fees charged for using the pier, and the track never got past the bankers. Moreover, there was opposition from local residents and landowners, and no locomotives were allowed in the vicinity of the houses, hence only horsepower could be used. Unfortunately the pier structure was deemed unsound and large sections often broke off in storms.

Development of the town as a tourist resort and the arrival of the railway were the final kiss of death to the track. Stone could now go anywhere in the country by rail, rather than simply port to port by ship. The merchants' stone yards moved to the station. Traders of coal, fish and timber continued to use the tramway and old pier for a time. The present amusement arcade along the Prom acted as a depot for fish and coal, as well as a morgue for shipwreck victims.

Three paddle steamers being coaled-up from Pier Tramway trucks c. 1910. (From the J. Ward Collection, courtesy of Swanage Museum.)

Life as a Quarryman

It was often rather grim working as a quarryman – in semi-darkness with only a candle to light your work, using primitive tools, the ceiling dripping down your neck and the wet clay of the floor clogging your boots, pony's hooves and wheels. Yet it was an honourable trade, involving dexterity and producing a proud race of men. So much so that their wives were expected to wash them down each day after they returned home from work. Eric Benfield gives a good account of what life was like in his book *A Stoneworker's Story of Stone*.

Stone workers were often paid in 'Swanage pennies' – slabs of stone, which they exchanged with shop-keepers and pub landlords in lieu of money. Pubs like the Black Swan had their own bankers, a raised platform, now railed-off, at the front where it has been suggested that men deposited their 'pennies' in exchange for beer. Some quarrymen's wives never saw any real money and many families lived in debt.

Smugglers and quarrymen often worked in cahoots, the cliff caves affording ideal collection points for contraband, and the whims just as easily offloading illegal goods as stone to boats waiting under cover of night below. Another, above-board supplement to a quarryman's income was to go fishing first thing in the morning, then quarry stone the rest of the day.

Quarrying Today

The last underground quarry was worked by Harold Bonfield (the Bonfields being a family of marblers, going back to medieval times). Then machine-worked surface quarries took over and the few small quarries today are all open-cast. Only a couple remain in the parish of Swanage; the rest are in Langton and Worth Matravers.

Chris Suttle, a quarry owner who learnt the trade from his father, has worked in the industry all his life. His firm Suttle Stone Quarries has a site at California Quarry above the town.

'We can quarry up to 5,000 tons of stone a year. California Quarry produces Purbeck grub stone, mostly for polished flooring and paving. Grub is a prize stone, it's unique – here's the only place in the world you can get it. A lot of our other beds of Purbeck stone are sold for local building throughout the south of England. After the Great Fire, London was metalled mostly with Purbeck stone, so any restoration work is done in the same style using the same stone. Purbeck is harder than Portland so lends itself to paving and kerb. It's a thin-bedded stone, perfect for paving. It was used in the old days also as large stones for graves and became very popular and valuable.

We quarry normally between spring and early autumn, as the stone has a high water content when it's quarried, so the danger is if it freezes while quarrying it cracks the stone. Frosts are less severe now than they used to be so we can quarry through to October. Purbeck stone doesn't soak up water easily, but when it does it takes a long time to dry out, so we leave the stone up to 8 weeks in the stock yard before there's the likelihood of any deep frost. In summer the drying out process is quicker and you can work it immediately.

The skill of the quarryman lies in determining when to cut it, so the person digging the stone is very skilled. He also has to recognise beds of stone, to dig it cleanly, handle it carefully with machines, and test the stone for faults – if it rings like a bell it's good stone. Everything is bespoke anyway so we can't really cut in readiness.

We have five diggers including one excavator and one loading shovel used to quarry the stone. Seven men work the quarry – three in the saw sheds (where the stone is sawn and machine polished), four on the natural side (building stone, rockery, paving, etc.) It's hard work, starting at 7 a.m. and finishing at 5 p.m., and the economics are borderline. There are huge planning and environmental costs. These days the scale of quarrying in Purbeck is much smaller, purposely, as planners want to keep the visual and environmental impacts to a minimum. So economies of scale can't be achieved and we're unable to meet our full potential.

Stone endures and serves its purpose for years. Lots of people rally to stop quarrying yet also support stone buildings. About 20 years ago there were 120 people working in the industry and 20 local quarries; now there's only 4 or 5. We've lost the family continuation – father to son. It was a good living. Local authorities now want to provide cheap housing, but what we need is good jobs. The only way to do that is to support local industry.'

At the quarry site, Nick the site manager explained how they have left an open quarry face for people to come and view. Some of the layers have been weathered in the ground by water over centuries and the various layers represent approximately 140 million years of geological history. No wonder geologists come from miles around, including overseas, to view and study these exposed rocks.

This old quarry face at California Quarry shows the beds of Purbeck Stone quite clearly.

In the working yard, the quarried material is sorted into piles of different stone. All have their different uses and are taken piece by piece as required, placed on conveyors and cut to order. The more the stone is polished, the more the colour comes through.

It takes about 30—40 minutes to slice through a piece of stone this size using the diamond-tipped cutting saw.

Learning More

- **Langton Matravers Museum of the Stone Industry:** tells the story of the local stone industry, has information on geology, a reconstructed quarr and capstan, and displays on local history and village life, which change each season. The museum is housed in a former coach house and stable behind St George's Church. Open April to September.
- **Swanage Museum and Heritage Centre,** The Square: has displays on stone working, geology and the history of Swanage from dinosaurs to World War II.
- **Burngate Stone Carving Centre,** Kingston Road, Langton Matravers (www.burngatestonecentre.co.uk): if you want to do some stone working yourself, visit Burngate Quarry (opposite the turning to Worth

Matravers). People of all ages, from beginners to experienced stone carvers, can learn, develop and refine the skill of stone carving. You can also see local masons and sculptors at work. The Centre has been developed sympathetically with local wildlife; they were careful not to oust the resident bats and reptiles in the 19th century quarry buildings on site.

Dry-Stone Walling

Around Swanage there is plenty of surplus stone, hence the preponderance of lovely old stone walls. And some not so old. Ross Prior, a local professional dry-stone waller, built the walls of Swanage Waste Water Works next to the Pier.

> 'I also do road bridges, houses, stone-tiled roofs, fireplaces. I started working with stone when I was 12 – learnt it from my father Reg, who built half the houses in the Winspit Road area in Worth.
>
> The average dry-stone wall is up to 4 ft high and 18 inches thick. You can find all sorts of rubbish in the middle of some, but these walls won't last. To build a wall properly, you build the two outside walls, then the one inside, interlocking and tying in with the outside walls. Sometimes I cement the top to stop the rain getting in, as that's what really causes the

Purbeck District Council received a lottery grant to rebuild the old dairy shed at Burngate Quarry in 2008, using the original stones. Ross's fine workmanship should ensure this building, with its 2-ft-thick walls, remains standing for years to come.

damage, or in private gardens so that kids don't pull the wall down and hurt themselves. It's always topped off with stones "cock on end" (cock and hen) to stop animals and people climbing over and to keep some of the weather out. To build 1 running yard – both sides of a complete piece of wall – takes a couple of hours. These walls are full of mice.'

A rich variety of walling styles are found in specific parts of the country, and Dorset diagonal coursing is peculiar to Dorset.

Graham Marsh's wall along the Acton road shows the distinctive style of Dorset diagonal coursing. The stones are laid at an angle to stop sheep scaling the wall and to help water run off.

Swanage Brickworks

The brickworks at Godlingston has been producing handmade bricks using local clay and spring water since 1861. Chris Caruana worked there for 8 years:

'In the old days, wherever they found clay you had brick makers – all you needed was a kiln. The traditional method is a slow process. You dig out the Wealden Clay ... where the concrete ends at the end of the beach you can see the green-blue clay under the sandstone ... then mix the clay with water to give a soft workable material. Then it is placed on the brick maker's table, a piece is thrown into a sanded mould, the excess cut off with a wire bow, the mould emptied, and the brick is then placed onto the drying trolleys. These in turn are placed in the drying tunnels for approximately

1—2 weeks. Then they are placed in the kilns. The kiln temperature gives different colours – lighter near the bottom, black at the top. Deep reds are very hard. It's all pure product out of the ground. You then sand the mould to give a sand-faced brick.'

One reason the brickworks keeps going is that it offers a bespoke service, producing any shape brick you want. No two bricks are the same.

Useful Websites

www.purbeckstone.co.uk
www.stone.uk.com

The Sea

'The spray sprang up across the cusps of the moon,
And all its light loomed green
As a witch-flame's weirdsome sheen
At the minute of an incantation scene;
And it greened our gaze – that night at demilune.

Roaring high and roaring low was the sea
Behind the headland shores:
It symboled the slamming of doors,
Or a regiment hurrying over hollow floors. ...
And there we two stood, hands clasped; I and she!'

(Thomas Hardy, *Once at Swanage*)

The sea lures many people to Swanage and this chapter looks at some of the activities associated with it. Two key aspects of Swanage known internationally are diving and rock climbing.

Diving

Diving groups regularly come to Swanage as it is one of the prime dive sites in the country. 'The UK's oldest diving school', Divers Down on the Pier, has three dive charter boats, a training centre with professional PADI trainers, equipment for hire and an air- and Nitrox-filling station. Divers provide one of the main revenues for the Pier. Bob Campbell no longer dives but has some good stories connected with the area:

'Divers Down ... I've been here since the start – I'm rather like a barnacle! I used to service all the diving equipment here. The Pier is a good nursery for divers. It's shrouded from light so you get a lot of life underneath, normally only seen in deeper water; 20 ft of water here is equivalent to 100 ft of deeper water.
There are two types of diving in this area: wreck and drift. A ship called the

Kyarra was torpedoed about a mile off Durlston Head at the end of World War I and is a popular wreck dive, but you only have about a 20-minute window when the tide is slack. Local fishermen noticed a disturbance of the tide and divers located this big wreck – it was very exciting, one of the most popular wrecks in the country. You can have 100 divers down there at one time and you still don't bump into each other! There are wrecks near St Alban's ledge and others scattered about the area. The Fleur de Lys, a trawler under Ballard, was dumped there after an insurance investigation. Not a real wreck and not my idea of wreck diving.

The other form of diving is drift. You drop in one side of the Bay and drift with the current. A surface marker float lets the boat know where you are. Some divers are looking for scallops or fish, others like me are interested in the geology of the sea bed, the coral outcrops and biology. West of Portland Bill there are some professional scallop divers, but none in Swanage.'

Bob is a member of the Historical Diving Society and for years has been researching, recording and restoring old diving equipment. He has a wonderful collection of old diving gear, archive material and memorabilia in Marine Villas.

A safe diving zone is cordoned off adjacent to the Pier, ideal for beginners. The Swanage area also offers 7-m-deep reef dives down to 30-m wreck dives. There's still cargo being brought up from sunken ships the *Kyarra* and *Aeolian Sky*.

The Isle of Purbeck Sub Aqua Club has about 55 members and a good social club. In winter members train at the Purbeck Sports Centre swimming pool; then as the sea warms up they use the sheltered waters under the Pier. They offer 'Try Dive' sessions and organise diving holidays around Britain and overseas.

Since 1995 divers have been surveying the seabed, mapping habitats, studying priority species, etc. as part of Purbeck Seasearch. Seasearch is a national project run by the Marine Conservation Society. Divers have surveyed pink sea fans, maerl (red seaweed), and mussel and eelgrass beds to help manage and protect these vulnerable species and habitats (see www.dorsetwildlife.co.uk for details).

Rock-Climbing and Wildlife Surveying

The cliff faces around Swanage are great for rock-climbing. Near the sea the cliffs are sea washed so any loose or fractured rock is washed away, making them quite safe for climbing. The dodgy bit is at the top where the rock is often loose. From the Globe westwards is a popular climbing area, especially below the lighthouse, and it gets easier as you go further west. Several natural inlets, e.g. Cattle Troughs, are good for learners, as are the quarry faces. At Durlston there are restrictions on areas and times of the year you can climb because of breeding birds. Glaister and Oxley's *Dorset Rockfax* book has all you need to know about climbing in the area.

Barry England is a local climber, sailor and Coastwatch volunteer:

'*People used to come and camp on the lighthouse green when it was unrestricted – maybe 40 or 50 cars. I've been rock-climbing since 1957, but don't do so much now. I installed the guillemot camera on the cliff-face at Durlston. It was a bit hairy with the camera and motor on my back. I went over the smooth boulder at the top, over the overhang, then was free hanging down to the ledge 60 ft below. It was a further 30 ft to the sea. We put the drill in and got pushed away from the wall, but managed to secure a steel plate and bracket, then mounted the camera there. It's made of aluminium so there's a corrosion problem and we're supposed to bring it up once a year. It's often difficult to get hold of a climber to do it. Katie Black(Senior Ranger at Durlston) is responsible for breeding bird surveys – monitoring how often chicks feed, what sort of food, number of eggs, etc. There's a live web cam on the Durlston website. One guillemot we named Tufty as he had a white crest on his head. He'd been coming back for about 14 years to the same spot on the cliff. We even had Tufty birthday parties with the children at the Centre.*'

Barry and his brother going over the edge to put the guillemot camera in place. (Courtesy of Barry England.)

There are other cameras – one on the Castle looking down into Durlston Bay where they've installed a hydrophone (waterproof microphone) to listen for dolphin sounds. (Barry commented that dolphin sightings have declined since 2004, probably because they are being caught in large trawl nets.) The hydrophone is installed on a quadruped approximately 6 ft high. Ed Harland, acoustics scientist for the Royal Navy, helped set it up. The steel was donated by the Swanage Railway and is heavily galvanised so it doesn't corrode much, though it's covered in coral and barnacles; hence the name 'Rolf's Reef', after Rolf

Williams, who helped install it. BT donated some marine cable and the Royal Marines laid it as part of a training exercise. The hydrophone has been useful in environmental surveys as part of oilfield exploration under Bournemouth Bay. It is still operational but is a struggle to maintain.

Birds nest on this thin layer of rock or 'puffin band' at the cliffs near Durlston. (Courtesy of Barry England.)

Sailing and Boating

To launch a boat from Swanage, you have three choices:

- the parish slipway by the Square (free of charge);
- the council Boat Park near the Lifeboat Station along Peveril Point Road (for a fee); or
- a launch point at the eastern end of the prom (which is chargeable).

Launching from the beach is prohibited. At the Boat Park, you may launch your boat and leave your trailer in the Park (cost £25 at time of writing); season tickets are available. The jetties here are for launching only, not for tying up, and fishermen have priority use of the left-hand stone jetty, which was paid for by the EU; the right-hand one belongs to the council and is open to all.

If you have a larger boat you must drop anchor in the Bay and dingy in. There are no public (visitor) moorings in the Bay, and boats tend to anchor at

Shep's Hollow under Ballard Down (unless there's an easterly wind blowing). Sometimes sailors cheekily tie up to a lobster buoy, then are surprised when they start drifting. Weekly tide tables are posted outside the Lifeboat House and the Tourist Information Centre on Shore Road and are printed in the monthly *Purbeck Gazette*. A 5-knot speed zone is enforced in the Bay. Swanage Water Taxi (tel 07802 480139) offers overnight moorings, a taxi service and hires self-drive motorboats.

If you are visiting Swanage, temporary membership is available at the Sailing Club (tel. 01929 422987). Sir Edward Heath opened the Club in 1996 when it was rebuilt – largely by volunteer members. They run a rota system for the bar, galley, safety boat, etc., with members putting in three duties a year. Barry England is a life member of the Club:

> 'We have a strong training programme for juniors, with two RYA instructors, cups and competitions. A family of four's membership is about £120 a year plus £60 berthing for a mono-hull dinghy, so it's very reasonable (especially compared with Poole). But with 500 members now wanting to keep their boats in the Park it has created problems. We have boats for hire and sharing. Temporary membership is restricted to sailing about three times a year.
>
> It's quite tricky sailing in the Bay, with the ledge at Peveril Point. We've lost boats over the ledge – they capsize and drift off into Durlston Bay. We let them go into calmer water, then pick them up. We tell visitors, "It's ok to sail in the Bay but don't turn right!" We always have safety boats out

The Sailing Club is exclusively for dinghies, but it also rents part of the seabed to provide members with approximately 20 secure moorings for yachts up to 40 ft, and recently this has resulted in more members joining with larger boats. (Photographer Simon Twilley.)

in races. Various reefs come out from the eastern end of the prom and by the Grand Hotel. Victoria Avenue funnels wind down into the Bay and locals use this in races – sometimes we tell visitors, sometimes we don't! The tide ebbs and floods very strongly. Swanage faces east and there are lots of easterly winds which pick the sea up – metre-high waves come into the beach, and it can be difficult to launch boats.'

Sea Rowing

Gigs were used by the Cornish in the 18th and 19th century to row pilots out to trading ships approaching from the Atlantic; the first pilot aboard got the job, so it paid to have a fast boat and strong arm muscles. Malcolm Turnbull, founder Chairman of the Swanage Sea Rowing Club (www.ssrc.org.uk), said that nowadays the gigs are rowed for recreational purposes and a thriving racing scene has developed, based initially in Cornwall, but now expanding rapidly. The Swanage Club was founded in 2001 and has several gigs of its own. Their aim is 'to promote community participation in healthy exercise' and they especially welcome families. Each year several regattas are attended and the club has a particularly successful women's section.

The Club has continued to expand over the years and 7 December 2013 saw the opening of a new, architect-designed boathouse. The building is cleverly landscaped into the hillside near the entrance to the Pier and, in addition to boat storage facilities, has six new rowing machines, allowing members to develop their fitness off the water as well as on. The launching of the gigs near the Stone Quay is always a source of interest to visitors.

Boats can be taken out by members at any time, so long as a competent skipper is at the helm. Both serious rowers and beginners can participate in the practice sessions.

The Pier

In 1859 John Mowlem constructed a wooden pier for trading: coal, timber and other materials came in, stone and fish went out – though only a small amount of stone as quarriers had to pay a toll to use the pier and voiced their objections to this by continuing to offload by horse, cart and toil. Moreover, the tramway built to serve the pier didn't last long, as once the main line railway linked up to Wareham, stone went that way.

There were other problems with the old pier. More paddle steamers were arriving with visitors, all vying for a berth. Picture those well-dressed ladies and gentlemen disembarking and having to wend their way through the hustle and bustle of traders, past smelly fish, dirty coal, slippery timber and dusty stone. Moreover, it was not very well built, and between 1895 and 1897 a new pier was constructed. Little remains of the old pier except some wooden piles adjacent to the new pier.

Unlike the old pier which had a tramway and no railings, the new one was much more user-friendly, with its wide promenade, shelter and proper landing stage for visitors. In the heyday of paddle steaming before World War I, about 300 passengers a day would alight at Swanage Pier.

In 1940 the Pier was viewed as a possible enemy landing stage so the landward end was removed as an anti-invasion tactic. After the War it was restored in concrete. Gradually as steamer traffic waned and the Pier fell into the hands of different owners over the years, it began to deteriorate and eventually had to be closed for safety reasons.

Then in 1994 the Swanage Pier Trust was formed and restoration work began. The Pier is now owned and operated by a charitable trust as one of only a few piers in Britain that does not receive any government grants; it relies heavily on the 'Friends of the Pier'

Swanage Pier is a success story – once again it provides a pleasant promenade and landing stage for boat passengers just as it did when first built in 1896, not to mention the angling and diving fraternities who make full use of the waters underneath it.

and volunteers. When you look at some of the costs of keeping the Pier going, you can appreciate what they are up against:

- Maintenance and running costs amount to approximately £200,000 a year.
- To replace a four-poster dolphin (the four-piled structure that prevents further damage should something heavy swing into the Pier) costs £40,000–50,000.
- There are 180 piles to maintain, some original; each new one has cost up to £18,000.
- The railings and lamp standards need repainting every other year.

In recent years the Pier had a good bite of the Heritage Lottery Fund, but it still has to rely on public funding and volunteers:

- Sponsor a Plank: this scheme has raised a considerable sum since it began, providing over 8000 brass plaques engraved with personal messages.
- Sponsorship of benches and lamps.
- Entrance and parking fees, which are modest.
- Subscriptions to become a 'Friend of the Pier' (minimum £12 for annual membership or £75 for life membership): in return, Friends receive a free strolling pass and newsletters detailing special events and latest news.

Repairing storm damage to Swanage Pier in 2013 at a cost of around £50,000, whilst general repairs to the structure are always ongoing and expensive. (Photographer David Haysom.)

Various companies on the Pier offer adventurous activities: Land & Wave (tel 01202 460440) – kayak fishing, bird watching and dolphin spotting; Pierhead Watersports and Ski School (tel 01929 422254) – skippered rib charter groups, wake boarding, water skiing, tubing and RYA powerboat courses; Divers Down (tel 01929 423565), Swanage Boat Charters (01929 427064) and Swanage Diver (tel 01929 423565) do what their names suggest.

Trips from Swanage

People used to go by steamer across to the Isle of Wight, the Channel Islands and Cherbourg for day trips. Travelling at a top speed of 20 knots, it probably didn't leave much time for sightseeing. The steamers often raced each other across the Channel.

> 'One of the fastest paddle steamers on the Bournemouth Swanage run, the Stirling Castle … had a disastrous record. In her two seasons, 1913 and 1914, she sank three yachts. In one incident, after pulling away from Swanage Pier and gathering speed, she swamped a yacht off Ballard Down and cut a second in half, drowning four of the occupants. The 270-ton paddler ended her days when she was sunk on war service in 1916.'
>
> (Ashley 1992)

A regular steamer service operated from Swanage until 1966. Today, the *Waverley* (built in 1947) is the last sea-going paddle steamer in the world and still takes passengers up and down Britain's coast, cruising the south coast in September and October and calling in at Swanage.

Blue Line Cruises (tel 01202 467882) and Dorset Cruises (tel 01202 724910) both offer day trips between Poole and Swanage. Dorset Cruises' boats can also be hired for private occasions, with catering and live music as required.

The Marsh family has been providing boat and fishing trips from Swanage since 1880. During the winter Roger Marsh is out in his boat *Freya* earning a living fishing for crab and lobster. Then from Easter and throughout the summer he uses his experience and local knowledge of the area to take people out in his other boat, *Precious*, offering general fishing and mackerel trips (all equipment is provided and you can keep the fish you catch) as well as cruises exploring local history, wildlife and geology. *Precious* leaves from the stone quay and is licensed to carry up to 12 passengers. Roger says, 'I can operate the boat on my own but sometimes nominate one of the passengers to help crew'. Look for the white board on the quayside or tel. 01929 427309 to book (www. marshsboats.co.uk).

Fishing

Jeff Lander is a fifth generation fisherman who fishes 12 months of the year, weather permitting, with his eldest son and brother helping out. He keeps his 8-m boat in Swanage during the summer and works out of Poole in winter when the weather is too rough to keep the boat in the Bay. He fishes up to 5 miles out.

> 'There are local byelaws on cockles and clams in Poole Harbour, and restrictions on minimum sizes on everything. We have to throw back any soft or immature shellfish which is necessary for conservation. We also have to put in a monthly return on what we catch, based on estimated weights. I fish full-time as it's my only income.

Jeff has 600 lobster and crab pots. These are in strings of 30, each string taking about 20 minutes to rehaul, empty and rebait. His metal-framed pots last up to 7 years, the plastic ones much longer; he buys replacements from someone on Portland. His father Alan still makes the traditional-style pots, only really used as ornamentation now that plastic and steel are available.

Steve Vince, former Coxswain of the Poole lifeboat, also fishes in Swanage:

Local fishermen work out of huts along Peveril Point Road, next to the council Boat Park. Most of the red buoys out in the Bay are either moorings or lobster/crab pots.

'I've got my own boat and fish on my own, anything from bass and mullet to lobsters and clams (in season). There are about four full-time fishermen in Swanage, including myself, plus a couple who just fish in the summer. We all work out of the Point. Our produce is taken to Poole, and we sell most of the catch to London, Barcelona and Cherbourg, and some locally. There are four or five buyers and we have to fight for a good price.

There are lots of restrictions, but no problem with fish numbers. I fish up to 3 miles out, but mainly along the coast and in Poole Harbour. The number of fishermen is dwindling and many have part-time jobs to subsidise their fishing. It's hard work and you lose a lot of days through bad weather. Then we haul up on the slip or take the boats round to Poole. Facilities in Swanage are poor – there's no shelter for certain wind directions so we have to move our boats around.'

The fishermen have their own moorings, and pay an annual fee to the Crown Estates (the Queen owns the seabed). Some locals fish from rowing boats as you don't need a licence; if you have an engine it's more complicated. William Chellingworth works at Field Farm Honey and in his spare time fishes in the Bay:

'You can fish anywhere, though inside the Bay is good for flat fish; bigger fish are further out – a mile or so. I catch Dover sole, plaice, bass, black bream and conger eel in specific areas. You can put down a pot any time of year, though April/May and September/October are best times. In winter the fish move out. I use different sized nets, but it's no good netting in calm water – the fish can see the net. I use a top net for bass, mullet, pollack and mackerel, a bottom net for bottom feeders like flat fish, etc.'

Rex, formerly at the Angling Centre (No. 6 High Street), describes the popular fishing scene:

'The Pier is a good spot as you don't need a licence for sea fishing – a few pounds gains you entrance to the Pier, then you can fish for free. In one competition, 21 different species were caught off the shore – trigger fish, and even cod are starting to show after 10 years. People go crabbing off the stone quay, by the lifeboats and off the pier. You can spin during summer, and lure off Peveril Point for big bass when you get the tides right – you need good footwear though as it's very greasy. The number of people who slip in...! (chuckles)'

The Angling Centre was originally the site of the old weigh bridge and 'Mr Charles Burt's Stone Office'. Here stone was weighed before being put onto the boats. The building also served as a booking office for the paddle steamers. These days you can book charter boat trips here. Skipper Tom bought his first boat when he was 16 and used to be the youngest skipper in

England. He takes holidaymakers and anglers on fishing trips up to 20 miles out, to Kimmeridge and along the coast. All equipment is supplied. Visit www.swanageseafishing.co.uk for details.

The Swanage and District Angling Club on Peveril Point Road has around 200 members. The Club runs shore and boat fishing competitions and especially encourages youngsters. You can keep an outboard engine there and use the Boat Park to store your boat (fees payable to the council, depending on boat size). The Club rents the beach from the council.

Peter Emery, a retired member of the Club, is down there most days:

> 'Within the Bay and straight out it's very safe to fish, but round Old Harry there's a nasty race when the tide is running hard. Towards the Point it's a bit weedy and rocky, so you can lose a lot of gear there. Bass feed on sand eels and you catch them with an imitation lure trailing behind a boat. Someone caught a Porbeagle shark around 200 lb, cousin of the Great White. Sometimes, once a year, they go out in a big boat to catch shark. If you need to know anything about angling in Swanage, just ask in the Club. We're very friendly and even help take hooks out.'

In the Club Room are a couple of posters on the wall showing the fish you can catch locally. Even the rare John Dory has been hooked.

Swimming

Jenny Hardy came to Swanage when she was 18. She is a fully qualified swimming instructor and lifeguards at the Swanage Bay View Holiday Park public swimming pool. One August Bank Holiday 20 years ago she swam across the Bay – from the lifeboat slip to 'the Chalk' (under Ballard Down), a distance of about 2.5 miles – accompanied by a friend in a rowing boat.

> 'The sea was at its warmest (20°C). Two weeks previously I did two to three sessions where I stayed in one-and-a-half hours or so as cold training. I used to do long distance anyway so the distance wasn't a problem. Friends coated me in lard, though I was skeptical, I just wore a costume. After the first hour and a half I was so cold I was beginning to lose any idea of anything except the fact that I had to keep going. Four sticks of Kit Kat and one-and-a-half hours later I made it to the Chalk. I probably should have taken a drink. I couldn't stand – because of the cold, not exhaustion. I didn't check the tide so it may have been against me.'

Jenny said she probably wouldn't do it again as the sea has cooled over the years and only reaches 18°C in the summer these days. Even so, she knows some locals who take a dip in the sea virtually every day.

Swanage has a safe bathing zone towards the eastern end of the prom which is roped off, and wardens patrol the beach in summer, though there are no lifeguards. The town has won Blue Flag and Quality Coast awards.

The Lifeboat Station

A lifeboat has been stationed in Swanage since 1875, and with such potentially perilous waters around the coast here, the Swanage Lifeboat Station is one of the busiest in Britain (out of the 236 around the country, it is usually in the top 10). They have a Mersey-class all-weather lifeboat (ALB) and Swanage is one of only three stations in the country that uses a slipway to launch the Mersey. The other vessel used is a D-class inflatable inshore lifeboat (ILB).

Jo Bowry, a former member of the crew, explains:

> 'Yes, the smaller boat is pretty hard on the crew in rough weather. We all carry pagers and you're on call all the time. Certain volunteers are shore crew who launch the boat. There's always a helm and two other crew members for rescues. On the big boat there are four core roles – Coxswain, Deputy Cox, Navigator and Mechanic – plus a couple of others up to a total of 7 crew. If you're going out to rescue fishermen you take a fisherman crew member. Some years we get a lot of boating accidents, others dog rescues – it seems to go in cycles strangely. We often have to do searches for missing divers, but they usually turn up safe somewhere the tide has taken them.'

You can join the crew at age 17 with your parent's consent. You have to show interest for 3 months, then do shore-based work for 3—6 months (launching and recovering the boats, washing down, etc.) and pass courses in sea survival, fire fighting and first aid. Then you become a full crew member and can go on to do other courses and progress as far as you want. RNLI Headquarters is in Poole where all the courses are held and new boats are tested ('So we get to play with all the latest gear', enthused one crew member). Retirement age is 50 for the ILB and 60 for the ALB, although this can be extended by 5 years with annual medicals and fitness tests for either boat.

The station receives no government funding and all the crew are volunteers bar the mechanic, which is a permanent paid job. Dave Turnbull joined the lifeboat crew in 1992 and is the Station Mechanic and Deputy 2nd Coxswain:

> 'Lots of people are involved with the station – in all about 50: from the ladies who run the shop, the Lifeboat Guild to the crew, medical advisors, launching authorities and Sea Safety Officer. The sea-going crew comprise about 26 of us and there are two shore crew – head launcher and winchman.

The Mersey heading out to sea. (Courtesy of Swanage Lifeboat Station.)

> *The six launching authorities sit between us and the coastguard – they talk to the coastguard when they're paged, find out what's going on, then decide whether or which boat(s) to launch (the coastguard has no authority to tell us to launch) and group page all the crew. Whoever's around turns up and we take it from there. We always make sure we have enough crew to man both lifeboats at all times.'*

On average, from pagers going off to the crew entering the water takes 8 minutes for the ILB and 10 minutes for the ALB – an impressive response time. At the station, the black boards on the walls list all call-outs since 1875 until 2000 (nowadays these are logged electronically). You can also follow them on Facebook and Twitter.

A good time to see the crew in action is during routine exercises – the boats launch every Wednesday at 7.00–7.30 p.m.

The ILB prepares to launch on exercise. (Courtesy of Swanage Lifeboat Station.)

The Coastwatch Lookout

In the early 1990s HM Coastguard reorganised their resources and decided to change to mobile patrols rather than fixed lookouts. All visual coastal watching stations were closed, Swanage and Holyhead being the last two stations to close in 1994. At that time, Ian Surface, the Auxiliary in Charge of the Swanage Coastguard team, approached the newly formed National Coastwatch Institution (NCI) with a view to opening the former Coastguard Lookout under the NCI banner. This was achieved with the help of a few friends and helpers, and Swanage was one of the first NCI stations to open in 1995. The current Lookout was built in 2001 following a successful fundraising appeal, most of the labour being provided by Coastwatch volunteers. Swanage Coastwatch is now one of 50 NCI stations around Britain's coast providing a visual watch for distress flares, overturned boats, divers, windsurfers, canoeists, etc., even illegal immigrants, any of which can be missed by more high-tech, sophisticated coastguard systems. The station is manned by volunteers, who put in thousands of unpaid hours and even have to buy their own uniform and equipment, pay the telephone bill and rent the building. They keep a log of all sea activities and local weather conditions and provide a vital and valuable service at no cost to the public (the NCI is a registered charity).

The Lookout at Peveril Point (old 'Perilous Point').

Coastwatch volunteers report to the Portland Maritime Resue Coordination Centre which instigates rescues by helicopter or lifeboat. They also liaise with the land-based coastguard in Swanage for inland rescues, e.g. climbers or dogs over the cliff; these people are on call but only paid for the time they put in during rescues. Local fishing boats are also often called on to come to the rescue.

Watch members Laurence, Ian, Tony and David describe some of what goes on in the Lookout:

> *'Often sea conditions are mild here compared with beyond Durlston as the Bay is sheltered. We calculate the tides and chart them; there are some very complicated tides in the Bay. We report our weather data to Portland, which uses clever software to calculate, for instance, where a body dropped over the side would end up. We monitor radio emergency channels 0 and 16 as well as some "working" channels and we can communicate with local and passing vessels on VHF channel 37 – there are lots of people listening along the coast. With the binoculars we read bearings which are then plotted on the chart and we also estimate distance to provide a position. Every ship over 300 tons and every passenger ship has a transponder that tells our AIS (Automatic Identification System) the position of the ship, how far away it is, its course, speed, dimensions, where it's going, etc. Some smaller boats have it too. We log everything we can ID. The Borders Agency is particularly interested if we see anyone jumping off a ship – not a common occurrence!*

The Lookout is manned 364 days a year, usually by two volunteers. On Boxing Day the blokes queue up to do the Watch (to get away from the family!) We have very devoted volunteers and fundraisers. It takes approximately 3—6 months to train – you don't need sea experience, you just have to demonstrate competence.'

Scouring the sea for anything unusual and writing up the log are two vital activities carried out by Coastwatch volunteers, in this picture Tony Kinsella and Station Manager Ian Weston.

Dangers

Strong currents off Ballard Point have resulted in 11 major shipwrecks (Wessex Archaeology 2004). The double tides, easterly gales and 'sinister ledge of limestone jutting from the water like crocodile's teeth' (as Hardy described it) together with Peveril Point and its dangerous tidal race means Swanage is not an easy port to berth in.

Easterly winds sometimes bring bodies into Swanage Bay and a number of divers have drowned. Peter J. Cooper mused: 'One Swanage past-time is coming out to watch the next catastrophe; it puts the town in the news every so often'. Certainly the police helicopter from Portland is kept busy rescuing divers and rock climbers – people either not coming up or going down too fast over the cliff. Poole Hospital has a decompression chamber for those divers who fail to surface properly.

The bay seems calm tonight
A grey sea under a pale blue sky
Swabbed and striped with purple clouds
The sun has gone down over the town
But a long autumn evening
Means it is not yet dark.
There is a long oily swell
Betokening something out beyond the Point.
The moon three-quarters full
Moving towards a September spring.
Round the headland
The waves are heaping up
In sullen blue grey masses
Heaving up channel
White maned
Eager to be somewhere.
They tear themselves apart
Along the rocks
With a dull grumble of disappointment
That they have not made it.
A lacy frill spreads out across the race
Like a Vandyke collar
On a navy velvet suit.
One of the fishermen
Tells me that he and three others have dragged up
A piece of wreckage
in Kimmeridge Bay
He says the Sun are paying them 200 quid for their story.
A woman and her son are walking
I pass on the gossip.
The Coastguard Search and Rescue team
Are hammering their pegs into the clifftop
Lowering themselves on ropes
An exercise whilst the light holds.
When I see them later in the Co-op
Shopping for the wife and kids
They'll say
"There's always somebody going over the edge."

(*Swanage Bay*, Peter John Cooper)

The Dorset Coast Forum and World Heritage Site Status

Geologist Malcolm Turnbull led the team that applied for World Heritage status for the Dorset and East Devon coast. Earlier, Malcolm had written *The Dorset Coast Today*, a detailed report that researched all aspects of Dorset's coast, and concluded that the coast's geology was of such scientific importance that it was worthy of special status. The detailed application process started in 1995 and included a comparative analysis of similar sites around the world. The 'Jurassic Coast' was finally added to the World Heritage list in December 2001. Malcolm said:

> *'Coastal communities understand that the sea and land need to be considered together. In 1994 we established the Dorset Coast Forum (www.dorsetcoast.com) as a better way of integrating the marine with the terrestrial in our approach to the management of the coast. The Forum is still going strong and we're very proud of it. It clears the air when there are conflicts of interest and it has helped pave the way for sustainable tourism. The World Heritage Site evolved out of the work of the Forum and, though designated for conservation reasons, it has helped raise the quality of tourism, i.e. interested people coming to the area with a respect for the natural environment. It has also helped increase the number of visitors coming out of season.'*

Swanage is the eastern gateway to the 'Jurassic Coast', England's only natural World Heritage Site. It is internationally famous for its sedimentary rocks of Jurassic and Cretaceous age (www.jurassiccoast.com). The Jurassic Coast begins in Studland Bay, near Old Harry Rocks, and ends further west at Exmouth, a distance of 95 miles, and is the only place in the world where 185 million years of the earth's history are exposed in a near-perfect sequence.

Smuggling

Smuggling brandy, rum, wine, tea, gunpowder, silk and lace was a popular sideline for fishermen and quarrymen in and around Swanage. Because of the nearness of France and the many caves and quarries in the area, it was a prosperous trade. It seems all members of the community had hiding places in their homes – secret trap doors, holes in walls, cellars, in the apex of the roof, under floorboards and paving stones – where goods could be stashed. It was so commonplace, and even the parson wasn't immune to a little illicit trading: 'Stolen waters are sweet' (*Proverbs* 9:17).

Smugglers often used the Purbeck Ridgeway, with Jinny Gould's cottage a useful half-way house for storing contraband, on their way westwards.

The cottage was isolated yet conveniently near a crossing of roads (the main Swanage to Studland road, under Curringdon Hill and not far from the Ulwell Water Works).

As the cliffs above Durlston Bay and the fields inland were honeycombed with quarries, with lanes going back far underground, customs officers and coastguards had a hard job controlling the trade. However, they did have the help of a revenue cutter, which patrolled the coast every night on the lookout for small craft. At sight of the cutter, it was common practice to throw any smuggled kegs overboard, sinking them near the lobster fishing grounds and fastening them by rope to a pot for later retrieval.

The Preventive Station on Peveril Point was built to give a clear view of the Channel and any illegal goings-on and to act as a deterrent. It was commissioned by William Morton Pitt and the buildings were completed in 1826, when it was leased to the Coastguard. The Station consisted of the Watch House and eight Coastguard Cottages, where the customs officers lived. These cottages were condemned in 1927 when four new cottages were built (behind the present Angling Club) and the original row of cottages became the Old Coastguard Cottages; since that date they have been privately owned.

The Railway

George Burt brought the railway, and hence the outside world, to the town in 1885. Besides being very popular with day trippers and holidaymakers, the new railway opened up a much wider market for exporting stone and really boosted the town's economy. British Rail took over the branch in 1948 and the track continued to be used by holidaymakers and local people commuting to work in Poole.

The Swanage branch line escaped the notorious Beeching axe – it was not earmarked for closure in the infamous report of March 1963 – but the first closure proposal by British Rail came just 3 years later in 1966. As car-ownership rocketed over the following years, the number of users of the service declined, and on New Year's Day in 1972 the railway was closed. Several months later British Rail contractors dismantled the track.

Determined locals fought the decision, forming a group to reinstate the railway. It was only through their hard work, enthusiasm and dedication that the town has a heritage railway today. Andrew P.M. Wright first got involved with the Swanage Railway in 1982 when he cycled from his home in Blandford to be a volunteer in the signal and telegraph department. He has been the Railway's volunteer official photographer and press officer since the mid-1980s:

WITHDRAWAL OF RAILWAY PASSENGER SERVICE BETWEEN WAREHAM AND SWANAGE

The Southern Region of British Railways hereby give notice that on and from Monday 3 January 1972 the railway passenger service between Wareham and Swanage will be withdrawn and Corfe Castle and Swanage stations closed.

Details of the alternative bus services are available at local railway stations and bus offices.

The news that caused such local public uproar. (Courtesy of photographer Tony Trood, from the Andrew P.M. Wright collection.)

'Most people visiting the Swanage Railway are probably unaware that the line has been rebuilt from nothing since 1976 and everything from track materials to locomotives and coaches have been brought in by road. Rebuilding the Purbeck Line has been an incredible story of ups and downs that proves the tremendous power of the human spirit against all the odds. It took British Rail just 7 weeks to lift the tracks back in the summer of 1972; it took Swanage Railway volunteers 30 long years to relay them.'

First Loco arriving at a desolate Swanage station in June 1976. (Photographer John Kellaway, from the Andrew P.M. Wright collection.)

The Railway Today

'In the old days, 10—12 coach trains ran on a Saturday, bringing holidaymakers from London (Waterloo) to Swanage. Now it's virtually all day-trippers. We carry about 200,000 plus passengers a year, which just about makes it pay. There's a small paid staff of approximately 50 – the core staff – and we rely on 400-odd volunteers. We really need to encourage young ones as without them there'll be no future for the railway.'

(Mike Streeter, Reservations Office Supervisor)

You can travel back in time on a steam locomotive between Swanage and Norden on weekends throughout the year, during school holidays, and daily from late March to early November. Their popular 'Freedom of the Line' tickets enable you to travel when you like, where you like and as much as you like during the course of your visit. There are 12 trains each day during the peak season (late July and August). A small charge is made for dogs and bicycles.

Along the 6-mile track you may disembark at any of the following points:

- **Norden** (just off the A351 approaching Corfe) – has car parking, a children's play area, picnic area, refreshments and toilets, plus the Purbeck Mineral and Mining Museum directly adjacent to the station (open on selected days).
- **Corfe Castle** – has the historic castle ruins and old village itself, Railway Museum and Exhibition Coach, Enid Blyton memorabilia in Ginger Pop, and the Model Village.
- **Harman's Cross** – a good place to start walks, has a car park and nearby campsites.
- **Herston Halt** – has a large campsite nearby and more walks.
- **Swanage** – has a railway shop and the Station Buffet.

The railway organises a range of special events throughout the year, including a Beer Festival and Diesel Gala, Steam Galas, children's character days and Santa Specials (very popular with families). Register at www.swanagerailway.co.uk for offers, discounts and a newsletter. At Swanage Regatta and Carnival time

The busy engine working area and turntable. A special viewing area over the bridge (walk up Gilbert Road, parallel with the track, cross the bridge, then through the gate on the right) allows you to see the action.

they put on a special Firework Train, with a Park and Ride facility at Norden open till late to allow you to commute to Swanage by train for the fun.

The Station Shop

The shop on the platform at Swanage is packed with railway treasures and open on all train-operating days and weekends throughout the year. The building was the old parcels office, an extension of the booking office next door, and the clock on the wall could be 100 years old. The shop is run entirely by volunteers and sells souvenirs, gifts, books and DVDs, to suit all ages. You can also pick up a copy of the Swanage Railway Magazine (published three times a year).

The Station Buffet and Wessex Belle

The station buffet is located in a fully restored carriage adjacent to the gardens and picnic area. It is open from 9 a.m. every day except Christmas, and also caters for groups and functions, e.g. birthdays.

The 1950s 'Wessex Belle' (evening) and 'The Dorsetman' (luncheon) dining trains both operate regularly throughout the year. Enjoy pre-dinner drinks and first-class dining while travelling between Swanage and Norden. The dining train is also available for private hire and corporate events.

Inside the station buffet

Helping the Railway

Now run by a dedicated team of over 400 volunteers and a core paid staff, the Swanage Railway is a not-for-profit organisation, with any revenue made being reinvested to preserve its heritage for the enjoyment and education of future generations.

Volunteers are always needed, whether to lay track, work on the locomotives or carriages, help out in the signalling department, check tickets, serve at the counter, in the shop or on the catering side – there's always a long list of jobs!

By joining the Swanage Railway Trust you can enjoy 25% off all fares and help support the railway. Locals may purchase a Resident's Card which gives half-price fares on regular services (excluding special events and dining trains).

It's dirty in there. Someone has to clean out a loco's smoke box at the end of the day. (Courtesy of Andrew P.M. Wright and Swanage Railway.)

If you fancy getting your hands dirty, the Railway Driving Experience may be right up your street. Alan Reeves told me how he'd driven one of the locomotives once, under instruction: 'We were approaching Corfe station and I was worried we wouldn't stop, but Peter Frost gave me top marks'. (Peter is one of the founder members of the Swanage Railway and now a driver. He used to ride on the steam footplates and diesel cabs from the early 1960s to the last train. The branch line, especially Corfe station, was his playground as a child.)

If you're keen to help and handy with a brush, there are always painting jobs to be done. The coaches are painted in Buckingham Green and the standard British Railway logo of the time appears on all the coaches and engines. A red stripe along the top signifies a catering coach.

The Future

In May 2009, a special charter train came down the track from Waterloo – the first steam locomotive passenger train to travel to Swanage from Wareham since the line was closed in 1972 – a momentous achievement.

The Swanage Railway has a very exciting future. Thanks to funding from the Coastal and Communities Fund, plans are now being progressed to introduce a trial diesel service along the entire length of the branch line between Swanage and Wareham in 2015–16. Then Swanage really will be on the map again.

The coming of the railway was perhaps the most significant event in the development of the town, so isn't it marvellous that this heritage line was saved from extinction and continues to be an interesting and important element of the town?

A brace of Standard 4s outside Swanage engine shed preparing for the day's duty. (Courtesy of Andrew P.M. Wright and Swanage Railway.)

Durlston

'Durlston' derives from the Old English 'Thurlston' which means 'the stone with a hole', suggesting that Durlston Head once had a sea arch something like Durdle Door, but this has been eroded away over time. Author Paul Hyland described Durlston as 'where contorted beds of the Upper Purbeck limestone stubbornly resist the sea'.

Thomas Hardy and his wife Emma often walked on the cliffs and along the shore. Hardy describes one evening sitting listening to 'On the left Durlstone Head roaring high and low, like a giant asleep. On the right a thrush...'.

Thousands of years earlier, picture another scene. Vegetarian Iguanodon and Sauropod and carnivorous Megalosaurus (depicted in the Swanage Museum and Heritage Centre) were roaming the Bay area. Internationally important fossil remains have been found here including a 130-million-year-old crocodile skull recovered by the Jurassic Coast Team. Also some of the earliest mammal fossils were found in Durlston Bay. Author Harry Ashley wrote:

> 'I am always happy on this Dorset Promontory, an ancient and still lonely place where long ago dinosaurs roamed, and had a most traumatic experience in this area in the 1960s. Dinosaur footprints were discovered when excavations were made above Swanage. I was given directions and ... climbed alone to a slight hillock and looking down the other side at the exposed layer of rock, I saw the footprints of a dinosaur made as he had plodded across what must have been soft silt. A cold shudder enshrouded my body as I realised that those prints were 120 million years old.'
>
> (Ashley 1992)

In 2001 dinosaur footprints (probably Iguanodon) were found at Swanage Quarries. The complete track is now on display at the Natural History Museum in London.

Part of the 280-acre Durlston Park was originally laid out by George Burt for the public's enjoyment. Burt acquired Durlston Estate with a view to developing the area and bringing people to Durlston to share the natural wonders: as he put it, to 'Look round and read great nature's open book'. He envisaged a new classy suburb of Swanage, complete with roads, shops, a church and tennis courts, but this never materialised. A good job too as the area is one of the gems of the area, offering great views, rare wildlife, spectacular geology and some unique Victorian heritage in the form of Burt's Castle and Globe. Indeed, as part of the education sessions now run at Durlston, Burt is put on trial by school groups as both lover of the natural world and destroyer (as a building developer).

After Burt's death in 1894, development stalled. At one time Durlston's major attractions were guarded by turnstiles admitting paying visitors only – not quite what Burt had envisaged. During World War II, the War Department commandeered the Park, mining and barb-wiring the whole area. Soldiers billeted in the Castle remarked that Durlston was a very different place then.

Gradually the area was neglected, the Castle left to dilapidate, until in 1973 the Council implemented Durlston Country Park, and things have been improving ever since. Money from the Heritage Lottery Fund and many other supporters was used to restore the Castle, create a new learning centre and provide facilities for special events and exhibitions. The Rangers and Friends of Durlston are working hard to bring Durlston into the 21st century.

'The tamarisks, their feathers
Fingering the breeze
The hawthorns like old men
Doubled up with age and sleaze
The cliff top grass as coarse
As Astroturf
Scuffed and nibbled to the roots
And rabbit dropping strewn
The thrift as bright as threepenny bits
Here and there discarded lumps of rock
And bits of brick weathered with use
From some forgotten installation
A quarry or a radar station
Windswept, watery, wintery Durlston
You may find this hard to believe
You are Welcome to wander the wonderful wildness
but come tea time you may never leave.

The bus pulls up but No-one gets out
The driver solemnly winds the indicator round
The walkers waiting in the wind
Mime through the window
"Is this the bus for Swanage?"
The driver shrugs and gestures at the sign
He has just put up
"Not on service"
And drives off down the hill towards the town
The walkers stare at each other
Windswept, watery, wintery Durlston
You may find this hard to believe
You are Welcome to wander the wonderful wildness
but come tea time you may never leave.'

(*Durlston*, Peter John Cooper)

Aerial view of Durlston Country Park. (Courtesy of Roy Egglestone, ex-winchman on Whisky Bravo Coast Guard Air and Sea Rescue helicopter.)

The Park is open all year, from sunrise to sunset. Car parking fees provide valuable funds to help maintain the Park for visitors to enjoy – whether you are walking the dog, flying a kite or wildlife spotting. There is no cycling or horse riding allowed.

Wildlife

Many scarce or uncommon wildlife species live at Durlston, and butterflies and orchids are particularly noteworthy. The cliffs are famous for breeding seabirds and the area is an important site for studying bird migration.

Birds

Can you spot any of Durlston's resident breeding birds – Fulmar, Shag, Cormorant, Gulls, Kittiwake and Terns? Durlston also has a very large winter Jay population (perhaps 40), which feed on Holm Oak acorns abundant in the Park. Other bird species occasionally seen and unusually prevalent here are Firecrests, Merlins, Redpolls and Woodcock.

Thousands of migrating birds, including Wood Pigeon and Redwing and especially Finches, are regularly counted at Durlston. The many evergreen trees in Swanage offer the birds plenty of overnight roosts, and an opportunity to feed and replenish their reserves. Good places to watch for birds are Long Meadow, the east side of the Castle, in Castle Woods and in the Gully which runs up from the Lighthouse.

The Black Redstart ('start' means tail; hence it is black with a red tail) is sometimes seen hopping round the rock levees outside Tilly Whim Caves. These stone ledges are also home to Rock Pipit, Jackdaw, Fulmar and Pigeon. Stock Dove and Jackdaw are all doing well here. Yellowhammer are in decline nationally but increasing at Durlston. Sparrowhawk breed here, away from public disturbance.

Boat trips are perfect for viewing the habitat of seabirds – Puffin, Guillemot and Peregrine Falcon – which nest in the ledges where the stone has been quarried out. You can watch the birds on the bird-cam in the Visitor Centre or on the website. The cliff path is also heaven for bird-watchers as you can be stood only a few feet above the birds and they don't seem to mind. The Gannet, Britain's largest seabird, is often seen out at sea. The open seas off Durlston are nationally important for Razorbill.

One of the largest Guillemot colonies on Britain's south coast is found on the ledges and caves of Durlston's limestone cliffs. Guillemot only come ashore to breed, spending the rest of their lives at sea. They nest in close-packed colonies in order to provide mutual protection from gulls and other predators.

Invertebrates

One of Durlston's more distinctive invertebrates is the Bloody-nose Beetle, which exudes an unpleasant-tasting liquid from its joints when disturbed. Lift a rock in a stone wall, sniff a pungent odour and you might be lucky enough to see the nationally restricted Bombardier Beetle scurrying for cover.

Drystone walls are also important habitats for hibernating amphibians and reptiles, including Adders. One of the best places to see them is on the south-facing walls above the entrance to Tilly Whim Caves; males like to bask here on sunny spring days.

Butterflies

Durlston mostly comprises natural grassland, where 33 different species of butterfly breed. Most noticeable are the Common Blue, rare Adonis Blue, Small Heath, Lulworth Skipper and Meadow Brown. Also the elusive White-letter Hairstreak is attracted to Durlston's elm trees; look out for adults perched atop the canopy of any of the larger elms in the park. Small Blue (which feeds on Kidney Vetch), Chalkhill Blue (on Horseshoe Vetch) and Brown Argus (on Common Rockrose) are often spotted. Every week between April and October, butterflies are counted along a set route.

Plants

You have to be pretty hardy to survive the wind and salt spray constantly thrown at you along the clifftop. Hence only specialised flowering plants, ferns and lichens are found here. European Tamarisk has taken a hold around the Castle and all along the stone wall below, as well as Cypress trees. Native plants to look out for are Portland Spurge, Rock Sea Lavender, Sea Aster, Rock and Golden Samphire, Wild Cabbage and Sea Spleenwort (the latter is only found between Chesil and Durlston and nowhere else in the world).

On the downland behind the clifftop grow Milkwort, Green-Winged Orchid, Early Gentian, Nit Grass and Lords and Ladies along with thousands of Pyramidal Orchids. Other plants to look out for are Wild Carrot in summer, Wild Parsnip, Fairy Flax, and Common and Lesser Centaury. Over 70% of the national population of Early Spider Orchid grows along the clifftop between St Aldhelm's and Durlston Head.

The small hillocks in the grass downland were created by ants (so don't sit on one!). The mounds are perfect for Wild Thyme and Eyebright to survive high above the thick grass sward which would otherwise swamp these plants.

Marine Life

A Voluntary Marine Research Area extends 25 km along the coastline from St Aldhelm's Head to South Haven Point. There are mussel beds off the Head and the Bay's rocky reefs provide a home for hydroids and anemones and are thus good hunting grounds for crabs and fish.

Because this part of the coast has rocky shelves, attractive to fish and marine life, dolphins have been seen, especially in autumn. Watch out for gulls flying directly above a school. A pod of Bottle-nose Dolphins used to frequent the area (mainly during the 1990s), but haven't been seen for some years now. If you want some comfort while spotting, the hut on the clifftop trail between the Globe and Tilly Whim Caves provides shelter.

Durlston is one of about 40 sites around Britain where dolphins are monitored. The Durlston Marine Project carries this out as well as studying seals and seabirds, mapping the seabed and managing marine litter and noise pollution. Events, guided walks and talks help educate and raise awareness of the delicate underwater ecosystem that exists off these shores.

Other marine species spotted include: passing Harbour Porpoises, Pilot Whales, Portuguese Man O' War (one can be seen at Kimmeridge Marine Centre), Common and Atlantic Grey Seals, Basking Sharks and Ocean Sunfish. The latter is thought to be the heaviest boney fish in the world, adults weighing in at 1 tonne. Some individuals are 3.3 m (10.8 ft) by 4.2 m (14 ft) across fin tips. They often swim near the surface. They feed on jellyfish and can ingest floating plastic bags by mistake, with fatal consequences.

The Visitor Centre at Durlston Castle

A good starting point for visiting Durlston is the Castle. The building was completely refurbished in 2011 to make it inviting and appealing to future visitors. Inside, old man Burt sits cross-legged surveying the scene. There are an array of free exhibitions and displays for all ages (some hands-on for the kids) on the wildlife and geology of this amazing corner of Purbeck. Meet the Purbeck crocodile during the 8-minute show 'The Rock'. A Ranger is always on hand and the Ranger's diary is a popular feature, listing the wildlife seen each morning at Durlston, while cameras bring live pictures of breeding seabirds doing their thing. I spent several fascinating hours rifling through binders of archive material on the local area, which are at the public's disposal. There is a wealth of information and Ranger Ali Tuckey was particularly helpful, though he modestly remarked, 'I'm the new boy, I've only been here since 1999.'

The Fine Foundation Gallery within the Castle hosts an ever-changing variety of exhibitions covering fine art, craft, history and science, as well as offering concerts and lectures and being a popular wedding venue. There is a water bowl for doggy visitors who are welcome throughout the building. The Castle is open every day (except Christmas and Boxing Day) and entry is free, making this an ideal part of a day out at Durlston.

The restaurant Seventhwave opens every day (excluding Christmas Day) and offers spectacular views from the café and terrace. Its walls are covered with the names of every species of living thing that Rangers and volunteers have recorded at Durlston over the last 30 years or so. Lifts throughout the building make the whole Castle really easy to get around. Take a twirl up the spiral iron staircase to the Belvedere Room, which offers seating, a selection of natural science books and roof-top views of Old Harry. Outside the Castle, picnic tables and bench steps are ideal for sitting and taking in the seascape.

Burt loved to celebrate the natural world in astronomical and poetic inscriptions on stone tablets about the place. On the battlements and turrets are a sundial, some global statistics and maps. Modern artworks such as the 'Timeline' which now leads down to the Castle take Burt's spirit of enquiry and fascination with the natural world and give them a modern twist.

The Globe

What weighs 40 tons, is 10 ft in diameter and is a perfect sphere? Picture Indiana Jones running for his life in front of a huge ball and you'll be somewhere close. It's the famous Globe below the Castle, made of 15 segments of Portland stone, constructed in Mowlem's stone yard at Greenwich and pieced together on site at Durlston, with granite dowels to hold the lot in place. Benches around the Globe mark the points of the compass. Rest awhile and clue up on your astronomy, philosophy and geography, though you might notice it's rather subjective (in true Victorian style, the Globe depicts the countries of the British Empire out of all proportion). Other slabs of stone around the Globe and Castle give snippets of information on the relative sizes of the sun and moon to the Earth, time differences around the world, the tides, and quotations from poems and the book of *Psalms*. Burt thoughtfully supplied two plain graffiti stones for 'Persons anxious to write their names…' Amazingly, they seem to have worked and the other inscribed stones are unmarked.

The famous Globe at Durlston. (Courtesy of Angela Bird and Dom Greves. Angela is an amateur photographer and conservation volunteer; Dom is a regular volunteer at Durlston and has been building up a comprehensive visual record of the Park since 2007.)

Tilly Whim and Howcombe Quarry

Tilly Whim Caves were both naturally formed by sea erosion and man-made by quarrying. The caves may have been named after the whim or wooden derrick used to lower the stone directly into boats below the cliff, and a Mr Tilly, who owned the caves. However, local historian David Lewer found no such stone mason on record and the triangular crane used by quarrymen was generally called a 'gibbet' or derrick, not a whim. So who really knows? John Mowlem as a young lad was supposed to have worked in this quarry. His nephew, George Burt, years later blasted through the rock to make an entrance-way for visitors to access the caves. You can see the graffiti some visitors left behind at the entrance. The quotation on the cliff face above the quarry is thought-provoking:

> 'The cloud-capp'd towers, the gorgeous palaces, the solemn temples, the great globe itself, yea all which it inherit, shall dissolve and, like the baseless fabric of a vision, leave not a rack behind'. (Shakespeare's The Tempest)

The caves were closed in 1976 after a rock fall and now provide an undisturbed home for bats. There is a good viewpoint just after the Globe.

Further along the path is Howcombe Quarry, where the Gully comes down to the sea. Here stone was removed by undermining. They blasted holes with gunpowder to penetrate the rock, then drilled small holes and drove in floor wedges, before cutting out the freestone. They then blasted the founder stone above, and you can see this loose pile of stone on the edge of the cliff.

Howcombe Quarry, a good example of a cliff quarry. Notice the dark bands of flint-like chert. Post holes can be seen on the lower ledge, where the gibbet crane would have stood, supported on its timber posts. There is also a fossilised ammonite on the ledge above.

The Lighthouse and Round Down

One of the best views of Dorset's varied coastline opens up westwards from the Lighthouse. It is one of only two lighthouses in Dorset built in 1881 some years after the *Wild Wave* was shipwrecked in 1875.

Anvil Point Lighthouse. (Photographer Dom Greves.)

A little further along from the Lighthouse, the foundations of a signal tower on Round Down are testament to the importance of the site in defending the south coast during the Napoleonic Wars. It was one of many signal towers (there was another on Ballard Down) erected to thwart the French invasion.

Back along the cliff towards the car park is an old quarry with reconstructed capstan. The two tall metal towers a little further on are measured mile markers, put up by the Admiralty in 1913 to test its battleships.

Walking Trails

'I've been coming to Durlston for 30 years and am still amazed to discover areas I didn't know existed!' This is not an unusual comment from visitors. If you want some direction, pick up a Durlston Trails Pack from the Castle – each walk looks at a different aspect of the Park. To help direct you, use Burt's original pointing hands on the stone tablets. The Victorian Trail offers a fascinating waymarked route from Swanage Railway to Durlston and vice versa and leaflets are available for a small charge from the Castle, Railway, Heritage Centre and TIC.

The Rangers also lead walks, looking at the wildlife and natural environment. So too do local people, such as Trev Haysom, who impart a wealth of knowledge pertaining to particular aspects of the area.

Local Fare

Markets

- Country market: Mowlem Theatre, every Friday, 10—11.30 a.m.
- Town market: main beach car park, Victoria Avenue, Easter to October, every Tuesday, 8 a.m. to 3 p.m. General stalls, bric-a-brac and farmers' market.
- Purbeck Products Market: Commercial Road, second Saturday of every month, 9 a.m. to 1 p.m. Order your Sunday joint direct from a farmer or talk vegetables with local growers.

Purbeck Products, www.purbeckproducts.co.uk

In 2000 a group of local farmers got together to set up a cooperative – Purbeck Products. The following year, foot and mouth disease stopped them dead, but again  in 2005 they pushed forward. With the help of the Keystone Project and its aim of raising public awareness of the local environment, the group really got underway, offering a diverse range of products, including meats, fish, vegetables, bread, flour and preserves. They sell their produce monthly at the market, straight from the farm or premises, and direct to campsites and other local outlets. They also offer farm open days and are often found at local events promoting Purbeck Products.

To be part of the group you have to produce within the Purbeck District Council area, be in an environmental scheme (entry level or higher), be Farm Assured if you have livestock, or source as much of your produce from within Purbeck as possible. It is important to farm environmentally, not necessarily organically, though some members are certified organic. The group works very much as a team, supporting each other.

Some Local Producers/Retailers

The producers/retailers described below are found in Swanage or very close to it; other local producers are listed in the Purbeck Food and Drink Producers' Directory.

Kathryn Best, Church Farm, Church Knowle

Since 1992 Kathryn and her husband Mike have run Church Farm. Kathryn shepherds for other people as well as running her own flock of about 150 ewes. Her Poll Dorsets are a local breed of sheep which (unusually) can lamb any time of year – a hardy breed and good mothers. All lambs are finished on the farm and sold before 12 months old. Her lamb sausages flavoured with different ingredients are very popular, especially with campers (she sells to local campsites as well as running her own site). Ewes 2—4 years old that haven't bred or are not right for some reason are killed, hung for 2 weeks so that the meat is tender, and sold as mutton – cooked slowly it is tastier than lamb. She also makes jam using her own crab apples, damsons and plums and any fruit given to her. She takes direct orders (tel. 01929 480151) and is usually at the monthly market.

Cedar Organic, Rempstone Farm, Rempstone

In 2007 Andrew and Claire Head took over Rempstone Farm and have turned it into a growing concern, selling organic meat and eggs. They set up their business, Cedar Organic, from scratch and seem to be going from strength to strength.

'We took over 530 acres of beautiful, varied Purbeck farmland in September 2007 and immediately converted it to organic. The farm includes three SSSIs – about 50 acres of heathland and a mile stretch of the Purbeck Ridge chalk downland, from Nine Barrow Down to Challow Hill. We graze ponies to help maintain the sward and eat young gorse and we control other invasive species by cutting. The wet and dry heathland supports four types of heather, Marsh Gentian and a rare Bog Rush, as well as lots of butterfly species.

On the farm we run a herd of pedigree North Devon Ruby Red beef cattle – our one bull spends half his time with the spring calving group of cows, half with the autumn calvers, so we have calves born at two times in the year, spreading the supply of beef. We run about 100 head of cattle at any one time and finish everything on the farm. Our flock of 200 Lleyn breeding ewes is expanding and we have lamb available direct from the farm for much of the year. Our 950 laying hens lay delicious eggs which are available in various local shops. We also rear table birds for meat: we buy day-old chicks, keeping them in small colonies of 150, free range from small mobile sheds, and slaughter them at about 12 weeks in our own small chicken processing unit. We have about 100 turkeys for Christmas, all sold directly from the farm gate. You can order from us (tel. 01929 481393, www.cedarorganic. com) or call in on a Friday 9 a.m. to 7 p.m. or Saturday morning. You'll also find us at the Purbeck Products market and Wareham Farmer's Market.'

Chococo, Commercial Road

Swanage has its very own chocolatiers, Claire and Andy Burnet. Passionate about fine chocolate, they started their business Chococo in 2002 and have won multiple fine food awards since for their creations which are made in-house every day at their chocolate shed in Wareham (their original chocolate kitchen in Swanage is now an on-site bakery for their café). As their chocolates and truffles are made with local fresh cream from Craigs Farm Dairy in Osmington and no preservatives, they should be eaten within 2 weeks, which is why you won't find their chocolates in any supermarkets.

> 'We only use the finest quality chocolate which is high in cocoa solids and contains no vegetable fat, additives or preservatives. We make all our chocolates by hand using fresh natural ingredients and the purity of flavour shines through as a result. Our chocolates are quite different to most sold in Britain which contain lots of sugar and preservatives, such as glucose syrup, which extend shelf-life. All our ingredients are locally sourced where possible (we're part of the "Dorset Food & Drink" scheme), and we source chocolate, which is ideally processed from cocoa beans to couverture chocolate for us to work with, in their countries of origin, including Venezuela, Grenada, Vietnam and Madagascar. But although we are totally serious about the quality of our chocolates, we have lots of fun with flavour and we hope that all our customers, young and old, enjoy their Chococo experience.'

They published their first cookbook in 2011. Next door to the shop in Commercial Road is their cafe. They also offer a nationwide mail order service (www.chococo.co.uk), workshops in school holidays, birthday parties and seasonal gifts. They expanded in 2013, opening their second shop and cafe in Winchester. Once tasted, you'll be back for more.

Field Honey Farms, Rempstone

Former chairman of the Professional Beekeepers Association, Robert Field has been a commercial beekeeper since 1983. He keeps 500 hives across Wiltshire and Dorset, including local heaths along Poole Harbour, gathering honey in spring and summer. He explains:

> 'Different plants yield honey at different times so it pays to spread your hives around so you don't rely on just one crop – all honey crops are very weather dependent. You just need permission from a landowner to site an apiary. Traditionally we pay landowners in honey – one jar per hive per year. This is a well-established benchmark dating back years; you put aside quality honey for your landlords.
> There's a real mix of different heathers on Dorset heathland. Ling heather

honey is the most sought after, but I also gather honey from bell and cross-leaved heather. Commercial beekeeping is a dying art and in many ways we don't have many competitors – they're more colleagues. We don't operate in each others' territories.'

Field Honey Farms processes and bottles honey from a purpose-built facility at Rempstone. They produce up to 25 tonnes of honey a year, a third of which is sold to local shops and the tourist trade; the rest goes to other beekeepers and big honey packers such as Rowse Honey in Oxfordshire, who package it as a monoflora honey.

Christopher Lees, Post Green Farm, Lytchett Minster

Christopher Lees is a farmer producing organic flour and beef. He grows milling wheat, and cleans, mills, bags and sells it direct from the farm. Many customers comment on the superior flavour and freshness of his flour in their homemade bread. The farm has signed up to the Food for Life Partnership whereby school children visit and learn about food and farming.

'I'd been farming conventionally for ages, but got fed up with the bad press farmers were getting as "destroyers of the world" (using chemicals, living off subsidies, etc.) so decided to go organic in 2001. It takes 2 years to convert, during which time you lose a good 50% of your crop yields. Now I'm a farmer that people appreciate and I feel good about this. I think it's important that people identify where food comes from and recognise that the countryside is where farmers do their work, growing food for everyone else. Purbeck is unusual in that there are still a lot of small-scale sheep and beef producers, traditional farmers who help maintain Purbeck as a special place.'

P. Loudoun, Wilkswood Farm, Valley Road, Langton Matravers

Wilkswood Farm is owned by the National Trust and everything on the farm is concerned with conservation and preservation of the natural environment, flora and fauna. Farmer Paul Loudoun keeps 150 cows (native Aberdeen Angus and North Devon) and 1000 ewes (Dorset Horns and crossbreeds), which he sends to the nearest abattoir at Sturminster Newton. His farm shop sells direct to the customer and he employs a qualified butcher to do the traditional cuts of meat and to home-produce the sausages, burgers, faggots and other butchery products. He also buys venison from the estate during season (autumn to early spring). The farm is run on a low input/extensive grazing system, and the meat is a conservation product – a result of the management of the natural habitat rather than the other way around (rather unusual these days). The shop is open Thursday and Friday 9 to 5 and Saturday mornings 8 to 1 (tel. 01929 427970).

P.J. and P.F. Samways, Langton Matravers

Farmer and drystone waller Phil Samways keeps pigs, beef cattle and sheep on a farm about a mile away from where he lives in Langton Matravers. His 35 sows and 2 boars live in straw pens in fairly traditional loose houses. On average one sow farrows each week (in staggered rotation) and the piglets are reared and sent to slaughter every 4 weeks. This provides a fairly constant supply of pork joints, bacon and sausages which he sells direct to customers (tel. 01929 439263 to order), campsites, farm shops and at the monthly Purbeck Products market.

Swanage Bay Fish Shop, High Street

Terry Dyke has fished in Swanage all his life and used to sell his catch straight off the boat and in the street. In September 2008 he featured in the TV programme Coastal Ways. Now he helps run the Swanage Bay Fish Shop with his partner Julia. The shop sells all Terry's catch plus a bit from other local fishermen and some bought-in from local markets – mainly in the Southwest.

> 'My great great grandfather originally came to Swanage in 1752 on a shipwreck, married a local girl and stayed. My family has fished in Swanage for the last three or four generations. Dad still works part-time with me (he's dead-useful for all sorts of things) and my son William comes out with me sometimes. We catch mainly lobster and crab. There's more fish around than there used to be, perhaps because there's fewer fishermen.'

Swanage Dairy Ltd, Unit 4D, Victoria Avenue Industrial Estate

Swanage Dairy has been serving local people since 1984 with doorstep deliveries and provides to pubs, clubs, cafes, hotels, etc. Den Williams and his team with their three delivery vans concentrate on the local area, to offer strong customer service. They deliver 7 days a week, offer 24-hour telesales (tel. 01929 427999), and can fulfill orders the same day, so you never need go short. They supply some Dorset-produced milk, cream, eggs and cheese; also yoghurt, butter, fruit juice, water and bread.

Jurassic Cottage Foods

Tina and Gary started their business in 2012 cooking up traditional English food like grandma would make. 'I didn't appreciate it at the time, but my mum was a marvellous role model. She made proper homemade food and I've always cooked like her. It's going back to doing things the old-fashioned way, using good-quality ingredients, no preservatives and cooking properly.' They support local producers by using local meat and vegetables and sell at Purbeck Products markets and food fayres. They can make things to order, providing individual portions to people on their own and supplying food for parties and other special events (tel 07951 033066).

Ashley Barnes, Purbeck Valley Farm, Harman's Cross

Ashley is a fourth-generation farmer working on the family beef farm. He has always shot rabbit and wild deer on the farm and in the surrounding area, supplying carcases to game producers. Lately he has set up a small business, Purbeck Wild Meats, from a cutting room on the farm, where he processes the whole thing as well as making use of pheasant and partridge from local shoots. He seems to be able to turn his hand to most things and, as a small sideline, his antler dog chews are great for canine teeth. He markets through Purbeck Products and direct from the farm (tel. 07753 266811).

Godlingston Manor Kitchen Garden

In 2005 Regula Wright started her own business with a friend, growing seasonal fruit and vegetables on a plot of land at Harman's Cross by the Steam Railway Station. Then she moved to Godlingston Manor Farm to establish the Kitchen Garden, growing fruit, vegetables, herbs and flowers.

Regula grew up in Switzerland enjoying a fantastic choice of home-grown produce from her parents' garden. After studying retail chemistry (involving a lot of botany and herbalism), she came to England to learn the language and later moved to Swanage to raise a family. Being a keen cook and wanting to bring her children up with the dishes she loved, she found the choice of seasonal fruit and vegetables in Swanage rather limited. She then took a permaculture course at Kingston Maurward and that was the starting point for her business.

Regula follows a crop rotation system and organic principles, using local seaweed, horse manure, green manure and homemade compost to keep the soil in good health. The hens and geese she keeps for pest control, as well as for eggs. She doesn't deliver further than Wareham as has more demand than she can cope with, working single-handedly, from sowing to delivery of produce, including supplying private customers with veg boxes, some chefs in Swanage, the Salt Pig in Wareham, Love Cake etc. in Swanage and Purbeck Products markets. From May to October you can buy direct from the farm gate. 'People appreciate seeing how their food is grown and where it comes from. My produce is especially popular with parents who want their children to grow up eating wholesome, non-processed food, older people hankering after long-lost taste, and trendy chefs'.

Folklore and Celebrities

Folklore

Folklorist Jeremy Harte wrote:

> 'On the Island of Purbeck the old road used to pass through a toll gate just outside Ulwell, and a cottage beside the road was home to the witch, Jinny Gould. She used to sit out on the gate at nights in the form of a cat, getting a lot of fun out of terrifying travellers, until one drunken carter picked up enough daring to land her a blow across the back with his whip. Suddenly the cat vanished, and back in the cottage Jinny lay dead (Luckham 1906). Today both the toll gate and the cottage are gone, although haunted gates survive elsewhere in the county. Normally it is ghosts which sit on these liminal markers, not witches, although a cat-witch is reported from a farm gate in Cheshire (Briggs 1970: B2.628). A Dorset witch is much more likely to take the form of a hare. One of these animals used to linger around the hills near Ulwell, teasing hunters by running in and out of range, but never getting hurt. Nobody had the cunning to load their gun with a silver sixpence, which is what men ought to carry when they suspect they are dealing with a quarry which is not right.'
>
> (At the Edge (No. 6, 1997),
> taken from *Roaring Dorset! Encounters with Big Cats*)

Another older local story concerns the **Agglestone Rock.** This landmark rock on the heathland about a mile inland from Studland is 80 ft round, 18 ft high and weighs an estimated 500 tons. Legend says that the Devil standing on the Isle of Wight hurled the rock (his nightcap) at Studland Church then being built – or Corfe Castle, depending on which version of the story you read – but it fell short. Hence the reason why the land behind Old Harry is called Old Nick's ground and the Agglestone Rock is also known as the Devil's Nightcap.

At **Old Harry Rocks,** a peal of bells is said to sound during storms. A ship carrying bells destined for a church in Poole was sunk off the coast, allegedly because of the crew's blasphemy. The spot overlooking Old Harry Rocks was described by Thomas Hardy as a 'windy, sousing, thwacking, basting, scourging Jack Ketch of a corner'.

The Rocks attract many stories. Some reckon the name 'Old Harry' comes from Earl Harold and his wife, who were transformed into the Rocks having been shipwrecked during a storm in King Alfred's time. Another legend is that they commemorate the medieval pirate Henry (or Harry) Paye. Paye, it is said, used to stand on Ballard Down waving a white lantern to lure French and Spanish ships to their doom.

Ghosts

In 1685 five men were hanged, drawn and quartered at Wareham following Judge Jeffreys' quashing of the Monmouth rebellion. As a warning to other would-be rebels in Swanage, their 'quarters' were unceremoniously dumped on the pavement outside Newton Manor (a mile to the north of town). The original flagstone was later taken up and still exists. A restless ghost is said to haunt the spot at Newton Manor.

Purbeck House, now a hotel, may have a ghost or two. A full-body apparition was seen in the cellar wearing a long winter cloak with the collar turned up, coach-driver style. When they dug the foundations for the new conservatory here, they found the footings of (possibly) a carriage house. Pipe smoke has been smelt occasionally in the corridor (former owner George Burt was a pipe smoker). Also some guests reported a knocking noise inside one of the bathrooms in the house, yet the room appeared empty.

The author David Leadbetter lives in Swanage. His book *Paranormal Purbeck: A Study of the Unexplained* describes nearly 70 locations in Purbeck, with contributions from over 100 local people. This book is a must-read on the subject. Specific stories relating to Swanage include buildings and people living in Gannets Park, the Parade, Manor Road, Cumberland Flats, Purbeck House Hotel, the Grange and other houses in the High Street, the Mill Pond, Argyle Road, Court Hill, Newton Manor, and Burnham's Cross near Godlingston Manor. There are also pages on Studland, Langton Matravers and Harman's Cross.

A whole chapter is devoted to one remarkably haunted location, the Royal Oak in Herston, which has had multiple phenomena reported by nearly 40 eyewitnesses. David says:

'When considering the paranormal phenomena at the Royal Oak, three points stand out. First, the sheer number of accounts and the variety of phenomena are amazing for one location and should help to convince those of a more sceptical frame of mind. The second point is that generally the most significant experiences occur not to the spiritualist, as some might suppose, but to other people associated with the pub, such as staff and

customers. Third, these people all appear to have a strong (psychic) link to the pub, which will be explored in greater detail in the concluding chapter of this book.'

The Red Lion and Ship Inn also have their own experiences of paranormal activity.

Celebrities

The town and surrounding area have been used as the location for many films, TV programmes and videos, among them:

- Musician James Blunt's video *Carry You Home*.
- The Style Council's video *Jerusalem*, set in Tilly Whim Caves.
- The last series of *Harry and Paul* (Harry Enfield and Paul Whitehouse).
- The Two Ronnies' silent comedy *By the Sea* (1982) used the town, Pier and railway station, Studland dunes and beach. Swanage Bay was known as Tiddley Cove.
- The Goodies' *Clown Virus* (1975) used the Lifeboat slipway and quarry at Winspit.
- Swanage Pier featured in *Wilde* (1997) starring Stephen Fry.

The character **Basil Fawlty** hails from Swanage. In the Fawlty Towers episode *Theft*, Polly tells Mrs Richards that Manuel is from Barcelona, but Mrs Richards thinks she is referring to Basil. Manuel says, 'No, no, he's from Swanage'.

Jonathan Ross has a farmhouse in Swanage, allegedly the biggest plot in the town, earning him the nickname 'Squire Ross'.

The following authors were also attracted to Swanage:

- **Thomas Hardy** wrote poems about Swanage and even set one of his novels, *The Hand of Ethelberta*, here.
- **Enid Blyton** was a regular visitor and many of her Famous Five adventure stories took place around Swanage (see the *Introduction*).
- **E.M. Forster** set about a third of the story *Howards End* in Swanage. Forster wrote about the enormous changes happening in Edwardian England and used Swanage as a metaphor.
- **Ian Fleming**, author of James Bond and *Chitty Chitty Bang Bang*, was sent away to prep school at Durnford School (now no more) in Langton Matravers.
- In **John Galsworthy's** story *The Man of Property* (1906), characters Old Jolyon and Superior Dosset Forsyte were inspired by George Burt and John Mowlem respectively.

Paul Nash wrote for *The Architectural Review* during the 1930s. He ripped into the middle-classes, highlighting the preposterousness of bolting old facades onto ordinary places. These days we like that, but back in the 1930s it was considered by some, including Nash, as pretentious. Peter John Cooper comments:

> 'The unplanned jumble effect of periods and uses is part of the charm and character of Swanage. It has layers. The town was invented as a Victorian seaside resort, but it's not really Victorian as it's been so built on, added to, knocked down, replaced.'

Other authors and artists associated with the town include **John Piper** and **Graham Sutherland** (both of whom worked on the *Shell Guides* in the 1930s), **Augustus John** and **Minette Walters**.

Family Fun and Other Activities

(Photographer Simon Twilley.)

Durlston Country Park

The Park offers plenty of activities for families, with most things originating from the Castle. The Castle has children's activity books based on local walking trails, and does a lot with schools. The summer treasure trail and Easter egg hunt are always popular and during the summer holidays there is something going on every week. Their website www.durlston.co.uk details other events, which change from year to year, and the Park is accessible all year, from sunrise to sunset. Electric buggies and an off-road wheelchair are available for disabled visitors. No horse riding or cycling. See also the chapter on Durlston.

Swanage Railway

Throughout the year, various seasonal events take place. For instance, 'Santa Specials' in December offer a pre-Christmas ride with mince pies and seasonal drink for grown-ups and a present from Santa for children. Advance booking is essential.

Young people aged 11—16 have their own club – the Sygnets. As members, they are involved in running the railway and plenty of practical tasks and experiences. They meet regularly and take an active part in the railway's operations. See www.swanagerailway.co.uk for more.

YHA Swanage, Cluny Crescent (www.yha.org.uk)

The term 'youth' hostel is a bit of a misnomer these days, as you are just as likely to encounter people over 50 as youngsters staying in hostels. The Swanage YHA is a good example of a modern-day hostel in an old Victorian characterful building. It has a comfortable wood-panelled lounge and some rooms have a sea view. It serves Fairtrade coffee and uses Red Tractor accredited meat. The hostel is licensed and stocks local real ales. I can vouch for their generous breakfasts, and they also offer packed lunches and evening meals, as well as a self-catering kitchen. Really good boards in the lobby detail events, weather, local maps and information, and there is internet access. For families there is a games room, board games and children's activity booklet on sale in the shop.

The house was built as a private residence on the site of a monastery of the Cluny order (hence the name Cluny Crescent). It was originally owned by Sir James Anderson, captain of the *SS Great Eastern*, which in 1866 laid 2600 miles of the first trans-Atlantic telegraph cable across the Ocean. Anderson still has relatives living in the area. The steamship was designed by Isambard Kingdom Brunel, and her great launching chains are the backdrop to the famous Howlett photo of Brunel at Millwall in 1857, housed in the National Portrait Gallery.

The house was used as a Red Cross Hospital during World War I for soldiers returning from Europe. Then after World War II it became a youth hostel. The manager there comments:

> *'Many local people don't even know the hostel exists, but we cater for a lot of repeat visitors – summer families – especially in Carnival Week. We are cycle friendly and provide a bike store, and the car park takes coaches. There is also a separate field study centre with classrooms and a resource room for teachers to come and do their own teaching.'*

Education and Field Study Centres

- **Leeson House**, Langton Matravers (www.leesonhouse.com): this lovely old house and grounds is used by a range of groups (residential and day visitors), Dorset County Council schools (from Reception to A level), and geology students from universities (some overseas) studying the Jurassic Coast.

- **The Chatsworth Centre**, 35 Ulwell Road, Swanage (www.allnatt.co.uk): offers accommodation and fully taught programmes, from coastal geography to environmental art to climbing on the local cliffs, for a range of groups from key stage 2 to A level, including youth group weekends.

- **Townsend Environmental Study Centre**, Cobblers Lane, Swanage (www.widehorizons.org.uk): a 6-acre site overlooking Swanage which runs residential, tailor-made courses in environmental education, biology, geography and personal and social education, which are achieved through learning outdoors, for a range of groups including key stage 2, GCSE and A level.

Where to Hang Out

When asked what's the best thing about living in Swanage, 26% of young people replied the beach and sea (Swanage Town and Community Partnership questionnaire 2005). The skate park at King George's Field in Victoria Avenue and the blue shelter near the amusement arcade on the seafront are also good spots for hanging out.

The Getaway in Chapel Lane (just up from the Purbeck House Hotel; tel. 01929 423421) is a focal point for Swanage's young people aged 11—19, offering sleepovers, trips, different sports, music (including a recording studio with live music and DJ equipment), environmental activities, circus arts, and an annual water fight, to name just a few things. Pick up a brochure from the Centre to see a full listing. It has a lounge and coffee bar too. If you want to try youth work, the Centre is always looking for helpers.

The Salvation Army, King's Church, Emmanuel Baptists and other churches also run youth groups.

Bollard Spotting

In the 1750s, there was a Royal Arsenal at Woolwich in London which housed great armament factories where guns and cannons were made for the army and navy. Defective cannons, and even some captured as spoils of war, were used as bollards to protect London's buildings from traffic by upending them in the ground. These proved so effective at stopping cartwheels from clipping buildings and damaging pavements and kerb that even when they ran out of cannons, they cast new ones in the same shape, complete with fake cannon balls wedged on top. They also acted as boundary markers.

Boats returning to Swanage after unloading their stone in London needed ballast, so George Burt avidly collected the old bollards and lamp posts that were lying about Mowlem's yards following repaving contracts and shipped them back to Swanage. In 1973, 111 bollard posts were recorded in and around the town, 40 or so inscribed with the initials of where they originated from. You might like to go on a bollard hunt around town to see how many you can spot, and what different names and emblems you can find. Don't forget to count those acting as gateposts in lanes and fields, especially around Durlston.

One bollard engraved with GPD near the old Lockup may have come from Greenwich Park District. Another near the Pier is obviously a former London resident.

Fossil Hunting

The best time of year to go fossil hunting on the coast is February/March, particularly if winter storms have caused landslips. The northern end of the Bay is a good place to poke around and you can walk approximately ¾ mile along the beach to the chalk cliffs under Ballard Down. However, stay clear of Durlston Bay, which is very dangerous because of overhanging rocks. The rocks which outcrop in Durlston Bay can also be seen in the many quarries on the Purbeck plateau to the west of Swanage and it may be worth asking quarry owners if you could look for fossils.

The Wealden Beds, which form the cliffs between Swanage and Ballard Down, also occur on the Isle of Wight where they are rich in dinosaur remains. Unfortunately very few remains are found at the Swanage end of the outcrop. Dinosaur footprints have been found in the local limestone (see the chapter on Durlston), and scattered bones, fish teeth and scales, turtles and crocodile fossils have also been found. The famous Purbeck marble is rich in the fossilised shells of *Viviparus*, a freshwater snail. Chalk consists largely of foraminifera, the microscopic remains of single-celled animals and pieces of broken-up shell, but occasionally larger remains are evident to the naked eye, such as sea urchins, fish bones and scales, sharks' teeth and gastropods (molluscs). The Castle at Durlston and Stone Museum at Langton Matravers have good displays on the geology of the area.

Geocaching

Thanks to Sue Gibbons for the following post on the Swanage blog 'Forum' page of www.virtual-swanage.co.uk (Sue also contributes to the online satirical newspaper *The Schmews* and has published a local newsletter for Purbeck parents of toddlers):

'If you own or have access to a GPS receiver, enjoy fresh air, exercise and adventure, then geocaching is something I really would recommend. Geocaching involves using your GPS to find hidden boxes containing an assortment of trinkets, usually of the Christmas cracker variety, along with a log book and pencil. The idea is that whoever finds the box takes a treasure, leaves a treasure, and records their visit in the log book. Most boxes are the size of an average Tupperware, but some – micros – are the size of an old 35-mm film canister. But of course the real fun of it is in the hunt.

To begin geocaching in Swanage with your GPS, simply register for free on the geocaching website http://www.geocaching.com/ and search for Swanage caches. There are more than you would think for a small town. Once you have chosen one to hunt for, enter the given co-ordinates into your GPS and away you go. Some caches are more difficult to find than others, and I always find an OS map comes in handy.

There are several micro-caches in the town – the ones I know are at the old Lock-Up, down by the slipway and at Sandpit Field, all containing just tiny pencil and paper. Bigger caches containing treasure swaps are found near the Globe at Durlston (fiendishly difficult to find this one is), by the Obelisk up on the Downs and at Rempstone, Dancing Ledge, Godlingston and Herston Halt. There's one by the Agglestone that I haven't managed to find yet, and if you look on the website you'll find plenty more in the area.

There is also a series of eight linked caches to find in Purbeck, where every cache in the series contains part of a code to decipher, which will lead you to a further cache.

Geocaching is not just a local phenomenon though, it covers the entire world. Geocaches are found all over Britain and in over 100 countries; worldwide there are around 800,000 caches hidden. But with its fantastic scenery, what better place to start hunting than around Swanage?'

Art for Free

There is a fine collection of mosaic and tile art on view around the town. Rod Humby's website (www.thejoyofshards.co.uk) has details and lovely close-up photographs (visit Rod's site to learn more).

- The Swanage Museum and Heritage Centre in the Square: Victorian floor tiles, possibly salvaged from the old Houses of Parliament.
- The Square: fish pebble mosaic.
- The Round House (the curved building opposite the Heritage Centre): mosaic flooring in eight shop doorways, each a variation of a fan design with chequered border.
- The Quarr Gallery, 17 High Street, also has a mosaic threshold panel.
- Beavers Restaurant, Institute Road has a block of modern tiles at the front, an inlaid doorway and terrazzo.
- Purbeck House Hotel: in 1869, Mowlem's unearthed a Roman mosaic pavement during the building of Queen Victoria Street. The original is in the Museum of London, but George Burt had a copy made in the entrance hall to his Purbeck House. The hallways also feature lovely mosaic flooring.
- Swanage Cottage Hospital, Queens Road: the name of the Hospital is set in mosaics over the entrance way.
- Youth Hostel: reception area.
- Look out for other collections of tiles and mosaics around Swanage outside private houses, in porches and along garden paths.
- St George's Church, Langton Matravers has an 'opus sectile' mosaic (a picture made from larger, specially cut pieces of tile).

Mosaic artist Robert Field lives and works in Swanage. His creativity is inspired by the natural world and can be seen on his website www.robert-field.co.uk and at the Quarr Gallery.

Maggy Howarth's beautiful pebble mosaic depicting three twirling grey mullet, commissioned for the Millennium. It is aptly placed outside the Swanage Museum and Heritage Centre which is housed in a former fish market.

The Swanage Seen Art Trail is a self-guided trail of paintings of Swanage by famous visiting artists. It was founded by local artist Carlotta Barrow, whose studio and sculpture garden are at the last house on Peveril Point. Download the tour map from www.swanageseen.co.uk.

Swanage Pitch and Putt

Andy and his border collie provide a warm welcome to everyone (including other dogs) at their 18-hole pitch and putt course at Kirkwood Park, Victoria Avenue. There is no dress code or booking required; you don't even need to bring any equipment as Andy has everything covered, including clubs for all sizes. There is even a special under-8s putting green. Among the greens and fairways of this 16-acre course are picnic places and refreshments, wildlife areas and great views, with the odd train to distract you as it puffs along the Swanage Railway track running alongside. The site is open Easter to the end of October. See www.virtual-swanage.co.uk/swanagegolf for details.

Putlake Adventure Farm

Two miles out of town in Langton Matravers is Putlake Adventure Farm (www.putlakeadventurefarm.com). Kids can let off some steam in the indoor heated play zone or outdoors in the play area. There are trampolines, sand cranes, battery-operated bikes and tractor trailer rides. The guinea-pig village and bottle-feeding of lambs and goats are popular hands-on activities, as well as all the other farm animals, including many rare breeds. Putlake is also a pet and garden centre retail outlet. They are open every day March to November and at other times out of season. Being a farm, no dogs (apart from guide dogs) are allowed.

Other Activities

Beach Gardens – one road back from Shore Road, open May to September and Easter. Tennis, basketball, putting and bowling green.

King George's Playing Field – between Victoria Avenue and the railway track.

Sandpit Field Recreation Ground – behind the Tourist Information Office. Crazy golf, children's play area and a bandstand.

Swimming – Swanage Bay View Holiday Park, Panorama Road (also has a sauna) (tel. 01929 422130), and Ulwell Cottage Caravan Park (tel. 01929 422823) – both open to the public.

Indoor bowling rink – Swanage Bay View Holiday Park, open May to September.

Waterskiing, tubing, wake boarding, powerboat courses, speed boat rides – Pierhead Watersports (tel. 01929 422254).

Amusement arcades – on Shore Road and round the corner from the Heritage Centre and Square at 6 High Street.

Regular Events

A decade or so ago, spending New Year's Eve in Swanage was a big thing, with posters on the London Tube advertising 'Come to Swanage'. People still come from all over to revel in fancy dress at New Year's Eve, when the lower part of the High Street is closed to traffic and parties spill out into the street. With 13 pubs, a host of bistros, cafes and eating places, and other amusements, people still flock here to have a good time. The number of other annual events is testament to Swanage's fun side.

Blues Festival (March) (www.swanage-blues.org)

During three days in March you can hear blues music at 15 or so different venues in town. With around 40 gigs, jam sessions and a full programme every afternoon and evening, the festival attracts a good crowd. Moreover, it's free – they just rely on people being generous when the collection box comes round.

Swanage Band Programme (May to September)

Musical performances are held at the Swanage Bandstand and Prince Albert Gardens throughout the summer. Pick up a leaflet from the Tourist Information Centre to see who's playing when and where. Music ranges from jazz, blues, folk and accordion to traditional brass or silver bands, played by any number of different groups.

Veterans Weekend (May/June) (www.swanageveterans.org.uk)

Across Britain, hundreds of events take place in support of Armed Forces Day, including the Veterans Weekend in Swanage. It's a celebration of the past and present contributions of our Armed Forces and veterans (so somewhat different to Remembrance Sunday, which concentrates on those who died for their country). Swanage celebrates with a seafront parade and displays of military vehicles and units, and drill and sandcastle competitions.

Wessex Gathering (June/July) (www.wessexgathering.co.uk)

Laura at the *Purbeck Gazette* let me in on a secret: 'It's impossible to find fancy-dress cloaks in the charity shops because all the Pagans have got them. There are a lot of Pagans in Swanage and once a year they have a big festival called the Wessex Gathering. I'm interested in Paganism, and I took my kids and we had a lot of fun'. Intrigued, I discovered that once a year in June/July a Wessex Gathering takes place, with workshops, talks, stalls, dance, music and storytelling. The website says '...we are not "affiliated" to any organisation and everyone is warmly invited who come with a good heart and warm intent'. The Gathering takes place at Burnbake Campsite, Rempstone, an enclosed, child-friendly site, and one of the highlights of the weekend is the big fireside celebration of the season.

Jazz Festival (July) (www.swanagejazz.org.uk)

Musicians playing New Orleans, Dixieland, swing, bebop, post pop, contemporary and traditional jazz, even 'bands that are definitely jazz but defy classification' – they all come to the Swanage Jazz Festival. Many fans of the weekend entertainment return each year and make a holiday out of it. Tickets are on sale from February. It's family friendly with under 16s free with an adult, and students get in half price. There's a Friday afternoon jazz cruise, Saturday brass band parade, and Sunday morning church concert of spirituals and gospel music, plus stroller venues.

Sailing Regatta and Carnival
(July/August) (www.swanagecarnival.com)

Carnival fun. (Photographer Chris Twilley.)

One week in summer is devoted to a euphoriant variety of events, including sailing races, gig racing, angling competitions, live music, firework displays, fun runs, sandcastle competitions, charity fundraising, processions, air displays, kayak racing, bay swimming, treasure hunts, a dog show and lots more. Book early if you want to stay in Swanage that week, and buy a programme to ensure nothing is missed.

Lifeboat Week (August) (www.swanagelifeboat.org.uk)

This is a fun fund-raising event organised by the RNLI. Trips on the ex-Swanage lifeboat run from the Boathouse all week. There are also angling club competitions, sailing club races, open evenings at the Lifeboat House, live music, stalls, build a boat race, etc.

Folk Festival (September) (www.swanageff.co.uk)

The Folk Festival in September is a chance to enjoy the last of summer at the seaside. Dancers, story tellers, street performers, singers and musicians perform – some freely; for others you need to purchase an event ticket. Or make it a weekend and buy one single ticket for the whole time. You can enjoy informal dance, music and singing workshops. There is also a programme of children's activities and events, including storytelling, street theatre and circus skills. If you want to camp, why not book a pitch at the festival campsite.

Purbeck Film Festival (October) (www.purbeckfilm.com)

The Purbeck Film Festival takes place over 2 weeks in rural venues throughout Purbeck, making it the biggest and longest running rural film festival in Britain. Discussions and notes add that little extra to the viewings on offer. Volunteers are always needed to help publicise the event and deliver and/or set up equipment.

Other Regular Local Events

- Lions Country Fair
- Rotary Fete
- Classic Car Display and Charity Day
- Swanage Railway events

- Purbeck Arts Weeks
- National Trust events at Knoll Beach, Studland (seaside scavenges, beach cleans, meet the Ranger, den building, etc.)
- Durlston Country Park events (including star gazing, woodland explorers, photography, quarry history, bird walks, Castle tour, activities for families)
- Burngate Stone Carving Centre
- Swanage and Purbeck Walking Festival – guided walks over 7 days catering for all abilities

See www.virtual-swanage.co.uk/events for a handy listing month by month.

Exploring

Cliff Place.

Walk 1: Around the Square

Start and finish: The Square
Approx. distance: 1 km
Terrain: Easy, all pavement

'The hotel industry in Swanage has all but died as people now take their holidays abroad. The hotels have been sold off as apartments and now it's mostly B&Bs, caravan and camping sites. Swanage had a revamping in 2000 to bring the seafront up to date – new handrails, street lamps, seats, etc. They pulled down the old toilets, revamped the Square, rejuvenated Prince Albert Gardens and made it an attractive centre. People have started to come back to Swanage. It's an old-fashioned seaside – people don't come for the high life, they come for the fish and chips and beach.'

(Chris Twilley)

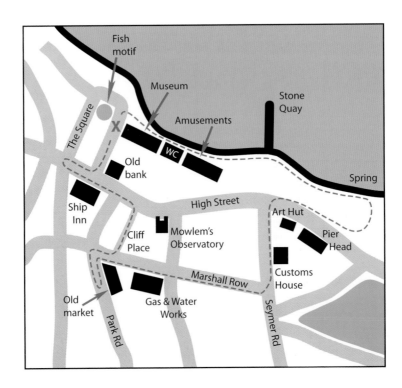

In the Square, the building that is currently New Look used to be a bank, but the old toilets to the left caused such a stink that staff and customers complained and forced the bank to move. Next door, Burt constructed a lovely, if little used, covered market, complete with domed glass roof. Unfortunately, the market wasn't popular and lasted only 5 years. The building was then rebuilt and used as a boat store, fish store and artist's studio. The Swanage Museum and Heritage Centre is now housed here. Take a look inside. The original floor has a slight camber on it with channels either side for washing down the old market floor, and the mosaics possibly came from the old Houses of Parliament. Children can sit and enjoy the jigsaws, puzzles, crayons and books while grown-ups take in the displays.

Q What was the name of the carnivorous 'big reptile'?

Q What is 'Our Donkey' of the stone quarries made from?

Come out of the Museum, turn right and head towards the old stone quay.

> This time I'm following the rails
> Buried in the ornamental slabs
> Where the stone carts once rolled
> By the soft slap of the waves
> Licking the crabs
> Against the quay.
> Fork off into a doorway
> I enter here – an arcade
> Of jittering lights and
> Electromanic music
> A portal to pleasure and to penury
> From the sealight into shade
> Push Past and out the other side
> Into a street
> Busy with pubs and bars and cafes
> Galleries and trinket shops
> And crowded with people living a life.
> I have travelled from here to now.
> The same place
> But a different place
> The same time
> But a different time

(*Rails*, Peter John Cooper)

A Water-pipe lagging

A Megalosaurus.

On the right on the wall of the Museum are some old arched windows. One has an information board.

Q What were the names of the boats used for stone loading?

The present amusement arcade was built over the old tracks as a covered depot for coal and fish. This building also acted as the morgue for shipwrecked bodies. Where the promenade juts out into the sea, look down at your feet at the carved paving.

Q What sea creatures and vegetation can you spot here and on your way to the quay?

You may want to pause and enjoy some locally caught fish and seafood at the open restaurant while you're here.

The stone quay was built in the 1820s on top of an earlier one constructed in the 18th century 'by the parish at a cost of some £300, the quarriers giving the stone and a day's work each' (Lewer and Smale, 1994, from document c. 1842).

Further along near the Pier, clear spring water gushes from the rock and across Monkey Beach. The beach got its name from the 'powder monkeys' (young boys who ran between the magazines and guns) who used to row ashore in small boats to fill up with fresh drinking water and provisions for the ships anchored in the Bay.

Across the road, a former bus depot, palmist, taxi hut and more recently Art Hut is now Old Harry's Locker, a treasure-trove of maritime curios.

The Pier Head Building next door started life in 1939 as a restaurant, became a temporary mess hall in the 1940s, and then later was used as a bingo hall, café and windsurfing school. In 2007 professional local artists Antonia Phillips and Nina Camplin (www.shockedcustard.co.uk) painted the murals, depicting the past, present and possible future of the site. Nina also painted the lovely murals on a house in Gilbert Road near the railway bridge. With changes afoot for the Pier Head Building, these frescoes will be lost but they will have served their purpose in possibly spurring on the redevelopment of this long-standing eyesore.

A The small lighters took the stone out to waiting ketches, anchored offshore.

A As well as shellfish and perhaps the odd fish in the sea, there are carvings of seaweed/coral and scallop shells in the paving, a mermaid and her catch near the open restaurant, and round the corner to the right a stone octopus.

Antonia and Nina's central mural on the Pier Head Building shows how it is inside, highlighting the plight of the building. The 'past' window is an interesting take on Edward Hopper's 1942 painting 'Nighthawks', with The Simpsons version in relief.

Double back and go left up Seymer Road. The large white building on the left is the Old Customs House. William Morton Pitt built this house, also known as the Rookery, in 1825.

Q What other purposes (besides customs house) did this building serve?

Now take a right into gravelled Marshall Row. This brings you out past the imposing Gas and Water Works building, and then to the junction with Park Road. Burt wanted to develop Park Road as a shopping and hotel precinct. He began by installing some high-class shops at the bottom of the hill, on the right as you look up; then, on the left, a market. The carved keystones around the bottom storey depict the wares sold in the market. However, the steep hill must have been a struggle for punters and traders as the area didn't develop as planned: '... these terrible gradients, more than sufficiently trying the occasional pedestrian, would be absolutely prohibitive to any likely resident, to whom they would assuredly prove a daily trial' (D. Lambert 1998, p.23).

A It was a library and shop (reference the plaque beside the front door).

Q From the keystone figures carved above the windows, can you guess what was traded in this old market?

Retrace your steps to Cliff Place and thus to the High Street.

After the War, a local chap went round the town cutting marks in the paving stones that had worn smooth to make them safe for pedestrians. You can see the original markings on stones away from the main thoroughfare, in places where nobody walks.

Q Look at some paving stones. Can you work out which have been re-scored?

Further along, past Park Road, the grub slabs cut by modern machine, with smooth, straight edges, show a good cross section of fossilised shells. They would polish up similar to Purbeck marble. The old stone pavements continue all the way up the High Street to just beyond Parker's (No. 205), where they become tarmac.

Pause and look back to the white castellated turret above the chimney pots. This was John Mowlem's observatory built atop his house. From there he could keep a close eye during the day on his firm's boats going in and out of the Bay and at night indulge his passion for stargazing.

Walk on to the Ship Inn. The stone bollards here were made by quarrymen. Cast yourself back in time and imagine standing here with the water lapping around you – beneath your feet lie the remains of an old quay and the land in front (now the Square) was once under water.

During World War II, Swanage suffered some bomb damage. It was nothing strategic, just that the town was on the Germans' flight path, and enemy aircraft used to drop any leftover bombs on the way home after their 'tip and run' raids. Some of Swanage's old buildings such as the Ship Inn took a hit.

A Beef, mutton, fish and eels, rabbits, fruit and birds.

A Stones that feel smooth and slippery have been worn by passing feet over the years; those with distinctive 'pie-crust' edges and scoring are not necessarily newer stones, but may have been remarked to stop them being slippery underfoot.

You are now back at the Square, the end of your walk.

Q What motif is etched on the Heritage Centre doors and depicted in the mosaic of the Square and surroundings?

After the air raid on 23 August 1942. The damaged part of the Ship Inn was rebuilt in similar style to its pre-war appearance. (From the Swanage Museum collection.)

A A trefoil of grey mullet, copied from the Victorian ironwork of the Pier (described and photographed in the chapter 'Family Fun and Other Activities').

Walk 2: Out to Peveril Point

Start: The Pier
Finish: The Angling Centre
Approx. distance: 2 km
Terrain: Slippery if you take the foreshore route, hilly over the Downs

Before setting off along the Pier, you might like to take a look at the foundation stone bearing John Mowlem's name set in the wall beside the second outfall pipe below the railings (when the tide is out you may be able to walk along here). It was 'laid in a workmanlike manner' by Mowlem himself in 1859, witnessed by Thomas Randall, Chairman of the Pier Company.

Dogs are allowed on the Pier on a lead, and there is usually a water bowl near the gate.

The white building on the Pier is Marine Villas, originally built by William Morton Pitt as a salt-water baths, billiard and coffee rooms, then later used as his private summer house. It now includes the Swanage Museum's local studies room, shop and maritime exhibition.

Just inside is a pictorial history of the Pier's restoration. Basil Buckland's collection of Donald McGill postcards is worth a look and you can buy comic postcards in the shop. 'The King of the Saucy Postcard', McGill worked virtually all his life designing postcards, even though his social observations and risqué

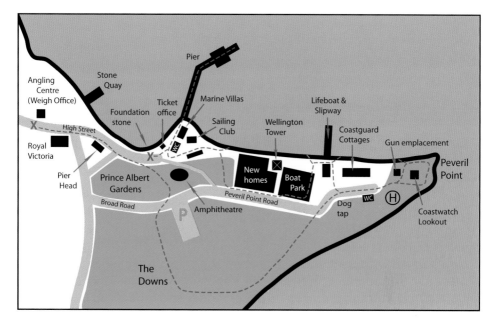

humour often got him into trouble with censors and watchdogs. In particular, he used colour boldly – bottoms and bosoms were often picked out in red to catch the eye.

Every pier in the country had 'penny in the slot' machines before World War I, and a 'What the Butler Saw' machine featured in the silent Two Ronnies film *By the Sea*. Use the special machine here to change coins for pennies and play them yourself.

The café is run by volunteers to help fund the Pier. The Maritime Exhibition (free entry) has displays on local wrecks, lifeboats, paddle steamers, diving and the Pier, and a lovely collection of model boats on loan from Mr A.G.L. Hardy.

> **Q** How might you earn yourself £1?

> **Q** In the model case, how many slabs of stone did the horse and cart bring to the rowing boat?

Back outside, you might like to walk to the far end of the Pier, a popular spot for angling. When you've had your fill of sea air, return to the pier gates. Turn left and you'll see the curved stone walls of Wessex Water's treatment works. They helped with materials to rebuild the Sailing Club and share the car park.

A As a reward for information leading to the conviction of offending person(s) who removed poles marking the new tramway.

A Eight.

Along from here is the area known as the Grove. The old Grosvenor Hotel dominated this sweep of the Bay, with the Clock Tower in its grounds. However, in the 1980s the hotel itself was swept away in favour of 32 new private residences, originally planned as part of a marina complex that was never approved. These look rather out of place next to the old Tower and most locals are rather scathing about them.

Go straight on past the water works and sailing club. If the tide is out you may take the slippery low-level route below the new houses; otherwise the upper path is always accessible.

The Wellington Clock Tower (on private land but viewable from the foreshore) is a misnomer as there is no clock. Imagine the year 1854 and builders in London are working on this Gothic-style memorial to the Duke of Wellington. They are surrounded by horses and traps crossing London Bridge, skirting the Tower which is positioned slap-bang in the middle of the road. Unfortunately the builders have run out of money and can't afford the statue of the Duke after all and even the clock doesn't keep very good time on account of the traffic bombing past (this is all the more ironic as the Duke was a stickler for punctuality). The Commissioner of the Metropolitan Police deems it 'an unwarrantable obstruction', and George Burt seizes the chance to acquire this

The Wellington Clock Tower, a Swanage landmark. At the turn of the 20th century John Everett used the Tower as an artist's studio. According to his diary, he fished from it too.

white elephant and relocate it to his home town.

Years later it mysteriously lost its spire – some say a storm took it out to sea, others claim it was an irreligious neighbour who objected to its ecclesiastical appearance. David Lewer in his book *Curiosities of Swanage* states that the spire was unsafe and so it was taken down in 1902/3.

> ❓ What creatures are hanging on to the Tower?

Past the fishermen's huts is the Lifeboat Station, open to visitors Monday to Friday between April and September. Guided tours are free, though donations are welcome. You can see the crew in action during training sessions on alternate Wednesdays and Sundays.

Next to the Lifeboat Station is the Old Watch House and Cottages. They were built in 1826 (according to David Lewer's book *Swanage Past)*, at a time when smuggling was rife. The cottages housed the guards and no less than eight coastguards kept watch from here and patrolled the cliffs in an effort to curb illegal activities – not easy with all those caves and quarries.

Tide permitting, pick your way carefully across the stones near the water's edge, or take the steps up between the Lifeboat House and Old Watch House and follow the road behind the cottages to the Lookout at the end.

Near the Lookout is an old World War II gun emplacement. It now houses some very informative boards telling you about the local area.

> ❓ Here you'll find something to keep the rain off.

During summer the Coastwatch Lookout is very busy logging the sea traffic going past, but at other times of the year you can visit the Lookout and see what they do. Barry England is one of the Coastwatch crew there:

> *'Through our binoculars on a good day we can see Calshot Tower on the corner of Southampton Water, and the flash from cars driving around the Isle of Wight. If we see jet skiers or canoeists going round the corner into Durlston Bay we report it to the Coastwatch at St Aldhelm's Head and also Portland Coast Guard. We often get asked "Can I cross the Ranges?" (referring to the Army firing range off Tyneham). They fire approximately 7 miles out to sea. We report anything suspicious, no matter how trivial, e.g. dumping stuff overboard, two ships coming together, and so on. We phone Portland Coast Guard as they could be smuggling.'*

A   As well as the roof, there's an umbrella stencilled on the inside.

A   Small gargoyles.

The large red buoy off the Point marks the end of Peveril Ledges. On Peveril Point, Purbeck marble juts into the sea and there used to be an open-cast quarry.

The Point has had a government – or quasi government – presence since the early 1700s: first as a coastal defence battery to guard the approaches to Poole Harbour. Men practised shooting a barrel moored on Tanville Ledge and divers still bring up the odd cannon ball from the sea. A coastguard/preventative and cliff/inshore rescue presence has been on the Point since the mid 1800s. The actual buildings have moved, coastal erosion forcing some moves but others due to changing priorities. The current Lookout is built on top of an old World War II bunker which was part of the extensive coastal battery built during the hostilities. There are remains of a building below the Lookout where the ledge is being undermined.

Walk back past the Hut towards the road, passing a helicopter landing pad on the way. There are some toilets here if you need them. The old coastguard building just further on has seen 166 years of service, but partly due to traffic problems in the summer, the shore-based coastguard has transferred to new premises at North Beach car park. On average they handle more than 100 incidents a year, ranging from animal and cliff rescues, unexploded ordnance and marine incidents to searches for missing persons and pollution events.

Go past the old ammunition store and on up the road, along the back of the old cottages.

Q What dogs are remembered at the drinking tap in the wall?

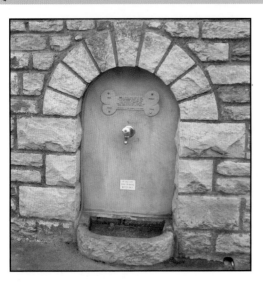

Take a short hike up the Downs for some great views. Prince Albert visited Swanage in 1849, arriving by Royal Yacht and enjoyed a stroll here.

A place for thirsty dogs.

A Ben, Fred, Penny and Tilly.

Q How much does a long-distance view cost?

Below is Durlston Bay. The former cliff-top path has slumped onto the beach and the cliffs are prone to rock falls, making the beach somewhat dangerous. Local John Beltram described how he'd taken the footpath between the blocks of flats down to a grassy ledge near the beach, and discovered some dinosaur footprints in a cleft in the rock. They were upside down – clearly indicating evidence of past rock movements ('... unless dinosaurs could walk upside down!', he joked).

Head back down the hill towards Prince Albert Gardens and the town.

Q Above the amphitheatre are some footprints. Who's been here?

These curious Tuscan stone columns came from London as ballast in ships and used to stand in the grounds of the old Grosvenor Hotel.

Amble down the hill to the road.

Q What animal companions has 'The Lady of the Rocks'?

Q How many whorled shell motifs can you see around here?

A Five (don't forget to look at the grills).
A A swan and a seabird.
A Dinosaurs and humans.
A 20 pence from the blue binoculars on the cliff top.

Head towards the Square along the High Street. Swanage has attracted its fair share of royalty over the years. William Morton Pitt took an old mansion here and converted it into the Manor House Hotel, where Princess Victoria and her mother stayed in 1833 during their West Country tour. Afterwards the Hotel changed its name to the Royal Victoria Hotel (naturally enough). In 1856 the young Prince Edward, later Edward VII, stayed incognito. Allegedly he slept on a sofa in the corridor before his identity was discovered, graciously commenting it was the best night's sleep he'd ever had. The old hotel is now private apartments. Picture Queen Victoria standing at the little window in the centre, waving to the crowd.

Past here, on the right, you come to the old stone weighing office, now the Angling Centre. To use the pier, traders were required to pay a toll. Many of the old stone loaders resisted by continuing to load ships in the traditional way, by horse and cart and rowing boat.

Q How much did it cost to take your hay and straw by horse-drawn wagon onto the pier?

Walk 3: Up the High Street

Start and finish: The Anchor Inn, High Street
Approx. distance: 1 km
Terrain: Pavement all the way, hilly.

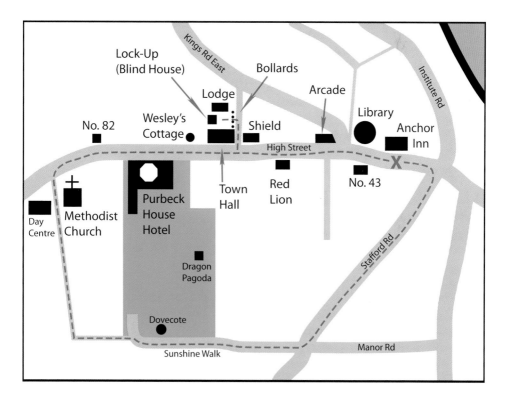

The Anchor Inn is one of the town's oldest buildings, possibly dating back to the 1600s; it sits next to one of Swanage's newest landmarks – the 1960s-built library. Local men sought refuge in the Anchor when the Press Gang was in town, seeking crews for ships out of Poole. Some dressed themselves in female attire to avoid capture. The Mail coaches would leave for Wareham from here and it was also the local market house where business was conducted, mostly by barter. It was also where you went to book the only bathing machine in town, which required a day's notice.

Opposite the library is a rather interesting building – No. 43 – originally a restaurant. Imagine sitting at this big arched window, which must have given a good view of the comings and goings in the High Street.

The Arcade (now Earthlights) was designed in 1895 by George Crickmay (Thomas Hardy was an apprentice of Crickmay) and was originally to have been the first of a row of shops. A portrait photographer Walter Pouncy took this first shop, hence the large windows and skylight.

As well as being an interesting building, the café offers a comfortable place in which to sit and watch the world go by in the high street. Choose from around thirty different teas and jackets straight from the potato oven, or peruse the menu, which has a brief history of the building on the back page. They have a good selection of children's toys, local books for impromptu reading, and are dog friendly. Local artist David Neaves comes in for his coffee most mornings and his pictures (which are for sale) decorate the walls.

The Arcade is a Grade II listed building.

Further up, the Red Lion dates to the 1600s when it was a farm with barns housing animals. Round the back is a garden and small children's play area. The pub is the informal committee room of the Durlston and Lifeboat crowd.

Burt's rival Sir John Charles Robinson built the block of houses to the right of the Town Hall. The stone shield on the wall came from Castle Mondolfo in Italy. Was this a bit of one-upmanship with Burt's Purbeck House up the road?

You can't miss the facade of the Town Hall – perhaps Burt's most exciting prize from London. Imagine you are in front of the Mercers Hall, Cheapside, in the City of London. It is the year 1870 and traffic is starting to converge on the area, necessitating the road to be widened. The Hall is not looking its best as the intricate façade, designed by Edward Jerman (not as it says on the front by Sir Christopher Wren), is covered in grime so they decide to take it down and revamp the front. Burt steps in, buys the original and ships it to Swanage to adorn his new Town Hall. Back in London, a replica is installed, but this takes a hit during the Blitz in 1941 and doesn't survive. Meanwhile, the good sea air of Swanage naturally cleanses the London grime from the stonework. So here we have another piece of original and unique old London to admire.

Notice how the Portland stone façade has a much cleaner look than the grey, dirty Purbeck stone on York Buildings opposite – which is why Portland stone was used for so many of London's fine buildings whereas Purbeck stone paved her streets. The lamp standards probably came from London. On the pavement in front, rather ornate manhole lids cover the coal chutes down to the cellar.

Swanage Town Hall. The Mercers' Company was a wealthy livery company, hence the carved drapes of cloth and central maiden, the latter being the symbol and coat of arms of the company.

At the Town Hall you may ask Reception for an information sheet on the paintings on display up the beautiful wooden staircase – all are local scenes by local artists and well worth a look. The receptionist may also be able to unlock the door of the Council Chamber Room upstairs for you to take a peek inside.

Back outside and left down Town Hall Lane is the old Lock-Up or Blind House. Originally this little gaol stood in the parish churchyard in the days when there was no policeman. It was erected by the Vestry 'For the Prevention of Vice and Immorality by the Friends of Religion and Good Order'. It was later moved to this courtyard when the church was rebuilt, to be handier for the town constable also stationed here. It was used mainly for overnight cases and it must have been quite sobering being confined in such a small, dark place on your own. The door is pitted with stones hurled by little hoodlums to vex the trapped inmate. However, some comfort was afforded as it was discovered you could insert a long-stemmed clay pipe through the keyhole and administer a drink to the 'prisoner'. I wonder how long it took the Vestry to work that out!

The old Lock-Up.

Burt appointed the town's first policeman in July 1851 and Town Hall Lodge on the right of the courtyard was formerly the police station. The townsfolk seem to have taken some time getting used to the idea:

'*Various petty annoyances and vexations came to a head on Christmas Eve, 1851, when at midnight a body of roughs set upon the man in blue. They mobbed him and nearly killed him, pressing him hard against the door of Mr Phineas Melmoth's House ... Mrs Mary Melmoth unlocked the door ... and drew the poor "Bobby" into the house. ... The mob, half shamed by this apparition, and half frightened at the possible consequences of their actions, fled precipitately, leaving the policeman in a sorry state.*'

(W.M. Hardy 1908)

Notice the peculiarly tall chimneys on the Lodge. It has been suggested that the original chimneys puffed smoke into the courtyard below and had to be extended to take the smoke away above the roofs.

Burt also gave the town a fire engine, which was kept under the Town Hall here on the left (imagine gates in place of the windows with the metal lintel above). The stone pump to the left of the Lock-Up has lost all its working parts – perhaps they went for scrap in the War or the pump arrived as ballast from some place else. It is unsure whether the metal pump on the right ever functioned, though a spring runs underground. Probably Burt sited them here simply for visual effect.

Retrace your steps to the High Street and carry on up the hill. On the right is a stone marking 'John Wesley's Cottage'. In 1774 Wesley is said to have stayed briefly in the cottage that once stood here at the invitation of Mrs Mary Burt, George's grandmother, who walked all the way to Salisbury to bring the preacher to Swanage. How could he possibly refuse after that feat of endurance and determination? Wesley preached in the meadow behind the Black Swan. The cottage was unfortunately destroyed in the War.

Who was John Wesley?

You now come to the Purbeck House Hotel:

'*... the home of George Burt built with all the durability of feudal times. Both in style and composition it lays emphatic claim to its "Scotch baronial" character...Devonshire, Peterhead and Aberdeen granite as well as Purbeck stone figure largely in this mansion which seems designed to live when all else in Swanage has crumbled to decay*'

(Land Agent's Record 1891)

Indeed its underground cellars were favoured by locals as the safest place to weather air raids. On the parapet above the High Street is an octagon tower. Inside is a plaque stating that a Roman coin was found while digging the foundations of new Billingsgate, and Burt's wife placed this under the foundation stone of Purbeck House for posterity. Let's go back in time to 1875 and imagine you are George Burt:

> *'Uncle John has been dead and gone these past 7 years and it's time I did the old house up, George style, for my retirement. What great timing – we just happen to be demolishing a lot of London and could use some old bits and pieces. Some of those granite chippings from the steps of the Albert Memorial in Hyde Park can decorate the outside of the house. At the highest point on the High Street, people can't fail to be impressed.*
>
> *I'll put the ex Millbank Penitentiary bollards in the stable yard and install a dog kennel to keep any riffraff out. Hope visitors notice the arched gateway – rather a good example of my early work (I'm particularly proud of my Neptune). Just to show I'm a cultured man, a bust of Shakespeare can go here too, with some carved grapes, leaves and scrolls – very à la mode. Up at the dovecote I'll install that old cartwheel – it's served its purpose carting my stone away and will make a great talking point as a table – a rotating one at that. For the Temple, dragons on the roof, floor tiles from the Houses of Parliament, Doric columns from the toll houses on Waterloo Bridge. The old statues from the Royal Exchange will add some dignity, but I wonder if the Mansfield Stone will last.*
>
> *The Italians seem to be taking an age laying the Roman mosaic flooring in my entranceway. Do they think I'm made of money? Perhaps then we'll be able to get the painters in to do the ceilings and the glaziers for the landing windows – our very own Christmas Story; the children will love it. Ah, there goes the servants' bell. Hardy's here for tea again. He always calls me the King of Swanage. Can't think why.'*

The Burts left Purbeck House after World War I and offered it to the town. After standing empty for 15 years, it was taken over by nuns as a convent and school. The convent closed after 60 years, but there is still a Roman Catholic school here. The house is now a hotel (note: children welcome but no dogs).

The hotel staff are amenable to you taking a quiet look round the public rooms of the hotel. The house has beautiful floors, painted ceilings and wood and stone everywhere. In the entrance hall, Burt had an exact reproduction of a Roman pavement (now in the Guildhall Museum) laid by Italian craftsmen; they took 3 years to complete this and other decorative features in the house. The result is amazing. To the left of the entrance hall is the former billiard room, once a chapel and now a function and dining room. To the right past the public bar is the servants' end of the house with a row of bells and a huge clock for time keeping.

Go back out the front door and left into the drive. The garden is a wonderland of hidden treasures (Burt was an original recycler) so once you have permission to explore the grounds, take your time.

> **Q** Just inside the gate, what might you find '...chained day, loose night'?

> **Q** Look up. Some horsemen are preparing for a procession. Why is this a good place for them?

Go on up the drive to Neptune's Gate. Neptune used to watch the comings and goings at Hyde Park Corner. Sadly he was struck by lightning and lost some of his whiskers and beard. *Go through the gate and explore the garden.* John, the gardener, maintains the grounds. The garden's centrepiece is a 90-year-old weeping ash, which has been propped up over the years. John explained:

'*The metal tubework and stone pillars were originally presumably put in to support the growing branches, probably by the convent people. I cut a couple of feet off its skirt each year. There are seven yews in the garden, about 50 years old. There's an old pond over there, but Health and Safety said we had to cover it. I love this garden – it's robust, mature, not fussy.*

As far as wildlife visitors, we used to have a badger sett at the end of the greenhouse. They would dig out pampas grass to line their sett, leaving a trail across the lawn which I'd have to clear up. We have a resident grey squirrel, and foxes walk through sometimes. There are lots of blackbirds. They're very good mimics – one managed to mimic a mobile phone, which kept me on the go for a while till I figured it out! A pair of magpies caused some problems. Prior to that, we had every type of bird come in, including wrens, redpoll, tits and finches. There's been a massive decline since the magpies.

There are still a few apple trees in the old orchard, probably original from George's day. We've planted a few new trees to make it more of a meadow. We plan to refurbish the old dovecote, and I've put the cartwheel in storage for now. Some kids deliberately broke the table, so I put the wheel in safe keeping and we've installed cameras. The angled windows over the sea give a great view from here. Below the dovecote is a slate water tank. Natural spring water used to be piped down to the water tower over the road, to the tank, and pipework came down to a cast-iron coke stove to heat the greenhouse and for irrigation. The chambers are still there but the valves have been turned off. The greenhouse is 90 ft long and all original. Even the

---

A A guard dog.

A Aptly they are in the area of the old Stable Yard. Imagine the coaches and horses arriving through the gates here.

window opening chains still work. The old vine has gone, but I'm nurturing the child of the vine – a new generation.

The old story was that after lunch the womenfolk and kids would play tennis, while Grandma sat in the Temple, and George and chums were in the greenhouse sipping brandy in peacock chairs.'

Q Past Louisa Lodge and the greenhouse, what do you think the grassed area was used for?

Now return to the High Street and continue a little further up the road. No. 82 used to be the New Inn and a popular watering place for quarrymen. It is not true what it says on the plaque next door, though it is a good story.

Q What is odd about the houses opposite (Nos. 99 and 101)?

From 1696, the Window Tax taxed houses according to the number of windows and openings they had – which fell peculiarly hard on the middle-classes – so canny homeowners simply boarded up some of the openings. It was not until 1851 that the unpopular tax was repealed.

There was a strong non-Conformist following in the town in the 1800s, hence the generous size of the Methodist Church on the left. It is a good example of Victorian Gothic architecture, and its landmark steeple perhaps deliberately outdoes the lower tower of the parish church of St Mary.

Q At the Sunday School, what does Jesus gather?

Take the small road between the church and Day Centre up the hill, then turn left along Sunshine Walk. This interesting alley connects homes and back gardens and passes along the back of Purbeck House, with some fine views over the town.

Q Who was here in 1858?

On reaching Stafford Road turn left. This brings you to the High Street where the walk started.

A G. Burt, aka 'Mr Swanage'.
A Lambs (children).
A They have fake windows.
A Croquet and tennis (notice the pair of ancient tennis racket frames atop one of the columns).

Walk 4: Around the Mill Pond

Start: The Black Swan, High Street
Finish: Purbeck House Hotel, High Street
Approx. distance: 800 m
Terrain: Pavements all the way, moderately hilly

The first thing you may notice on entering the Black Swan is the sweet smell of wood smoke and the pictures on the walls by local artists. In this friendly pub you get a warm welcome from Alyson:

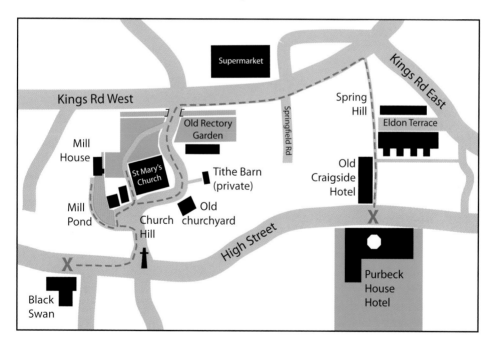

'The Swan was originally a coaching house and staging post for the Royal Mail and could be up to 600 years old. The Mill Pond down the road always had swans on it, hence the name I s'pose. We pride ourselves on good homemade food. The Swan attracts an older clientele and we have *a lot of loyal customers. People feel comfortable here. Our real ales get a constant thumbs up and our wines are extremely popular and not available in supermarkets.*

We host Shove Ha'penny matches for the Isle of Purbeck league (predominantly Swanage plus a couple of pubs in Worth Matravers and Langton). Longboard shove ha'penny is only played in the Purbeck and there is a particular style of board used. Every pub with a team has its own board. But we're finding it hard to attract new blood (the average age is 50+) so it's a dying game. It's very skillful, and we play every Thursday night through the winter.'

Children are welcome in the lounge bar or walled garden, and dogs attached to their owners are allowed in; there is even a box of dog biscuits under the counter. Outside the front is a railed-off platform. In the old days it is said that this would have been piled high with 'stone pennies' – the cut stone quarrymen used to barter for drink. Many inns had this arrangement, but this is the only one still with its railings. Hence the phrase 'I got stoned' perhaps?

Just down the road at the top of Church Hill is a cross which stands in place of the village pump, but the pump disappeared in 1907 when most houses went onto domestic water supply. It was erected as a family memorial to Sir Reginald Palgrave, brother of poet Francis Turner Palgrave. The family wrote the inscription in Latin so most people could not read it – their idea of a public yet selectively private memorial.

Some of the cottages here were built with traditional rubble wall stone and roof tiles. Notice the old sash windows on these houses.

Q What animal opens the door to No. 7?

Q Opposite can you spot something to do with a ship here?

Just to the left of the church is a tranquil Mill Pond. The pool has always been and still is fed by a spring, which you can see bubbling in the corner behind the weeping willow, and which formed the town's water supply for many years. Around 1880, it is said that locals were so fed up with having to retrieve drunks from the Black Swan who had fallen into the pond that they built a wall round the water's edge. Another reason could have been to stop the water being muddied by the cattle and horses that visited to drink.

A An anchor.

A A seahorse.

A mill pond has been here since medieval times.

The old **Mill House** was probably rebuilt in 1754, but there is evidence of a mill being here earlier. The mill and wheel have been silent since 1928. Wild mint grows down near the outflow pipe.

Q What do the ducks use to get in and out of the water?

Q When were the houses built here?

The base of the tower of **St Mary's Church** dates to around 1250. Fanciful stories in many books suggest it was built as a defensive refuge. It was said that locals climbed a ladder to reach the top, then hauled up the ladder behind them so that marauding French pirates, who often came raiding in the 13th and 14th centuries, could not get in. The storeys above were added in 1620. Out of the small high window in the east wall of the tower inmates could watch for and take shots at pirates; today it is more likely to be used to judge when to ring the bells at weddings. The oldest bell (dated 1594) of the eight in the tower is still in weekly use. It bears the inscription 'Thinke on God'. If you enjoy the sound of bells, there are practice sessions on Wednesday evenings, and if you would like a go you can sign up for a course in bell ringing. Notice any similarity of the clock to Big Ben? It was supplied by the same clockmakers Dent & Co. of London.

A 1888.

A A special wooden duck ramp.

The church was originally a chapel of ease of the parish of Worth Matravers, with the vicar making the regular trek along Priest's Way to minister to the smaller congregation in 'Swanwich'. The church has been rebuilt at least four times and parish registers go back to 1563. Organ recitals and other musical events are held regularly, especially throughout the summer.

Inside are many treasures worth exploring. Dorset artist Henry Haig's abstract stained-glass window on your left was installed in 1994. It depicts the Creation as radiating elements 'that become identifiable and open to exploration, but all spring from the wonder of growing forms, seemingly different but demonstrating similarities no matter what extremes of scale may exist: cosmic and microscopic existence in time and space emanating from the one source'.

Q How many angels are there above the altar in the Revelation Window?

Q What is the symbol and motto of the Royal British Legion (see above the gallery)?

The font by the south door (formerly the main church entrance) is of Purbeck marble. The cover was made in the Swanage Grammar School workshop, just before the school closed.

Q Framing the stained-glass window here is a beautiful 14th-century arch from the old church. What animals are depicted in the Nativity scene?

As you leave the church notice the two carved heads either side of the door, that of a king and bishop representing State and Church. Along the boundary ahead of you and to the right you may notice two iron bars which are all that remain of some metal railings scrapped during World War II. When the church was extended to provide a new north aisle in 1907/08, apparently the builders were able to put the old wall (facing King's Road with the round window in it) on rollers and wheel it out to save demolishing it. More recently a disabled access entranceway has been built and in so doing they had to disturb some of the old headstones, hence the pile along the wall here awaiting rehoming. Some old carved stones were used as slabs along the walkway.

Back up the steps towards the Mill Pond, turn left and walk down the road. On the right is an old churchyard. Some important families rest here; the small headstones with just initials and a date are those of less well-off folk.

A A cow, donkey, lamb and robin.

A A lion and 'Service not self'.

A Thirteen.

Most headstones in this old churchyard are illegible, some being more than 150 years old (the most recent inhabitant died in 1855).

The sawn-off column at the back of the churchyard apparently represents a life cut short and here lies Robert Burt, George Burt's father. George himself resides in Kensal Green, London, apparently *the* place to be buried in those days. London was, after all, where he did most of his business. John Mowlem's vault, originally at the old church in Kingston near Corfe, is now in the later cemetery above the railway station.

Leave the churchyard and continue on down the road. Down a drive on the right, the Grade II-listed Tithe Barn used to house the Swanage Museum but is now private property. The word 'tithe' means 'tenth and farmers had to give a tenth/tithe of their produce each year for the upkeep of the church and clergy.

The barn was probably used to store grain from the mill. The slits in the wall are said to be 'owl' windows – why do you think they were called this?

Below the church, pause for a moment at the Brook. There used to be a ford here. In the past the Brook used to flood, so a meter box was installed to

A Owls did a valuable job of controlling rats and mice and these small windows allowed them to fly in and out.

monitor the flow, and the water level is controlled higher up the course (where it splits off right into King George's Field). The Brook eventually enters the sea next to the Mowlem Theatre.

Turn right over the bridge and walk down the road, past the Rectory Garden. The metal bar across the Brook opposite the Co-op is probably a drain conduit.

Turn right into Spring Hill. On the way up, at the end of the path behind the cottages of Eldon Terrace, is a rusty scrolled metal post with a carving on top, the emblem of the Dorset Iron Foundry in Poole which built small locomotives. This post is one of many old sewer pipes that used to be dotted around town and it would have been much taller than this originally.

As you proceed up the incline the houses appear to get smaller and smaller, ending in The Vault, a tiny abode that was once the old boiler room of the former Craigside Hotel above, now converted into flats.

At the High Street, turn right and walk back to the Black Swan, or turn left into town.

Purbeck House Hotel.

Walk 5: The High Street to Townsend

Start and finish: The Methodist Church, High Street
Approx. distance: 1.8 km
Terrain: Pavement to start with, then nature reserve (can be muddy; great for dogs and children), hilly.

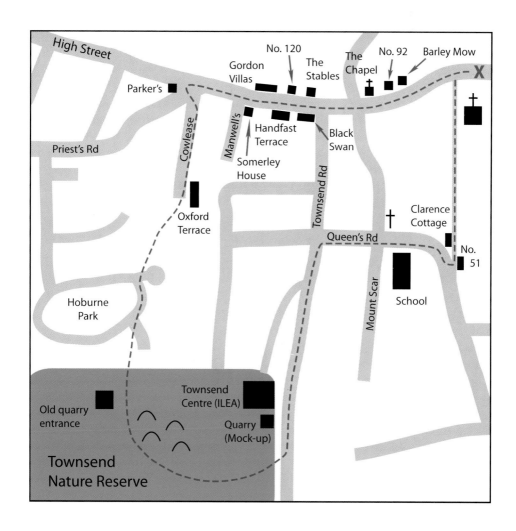

By the Methodist Church, where Walk 3 turned to go up the alley, is an area of town called Jubilee Square. Further up was The Narrows, so named because the street used to be no more than one wagon's width. Then the whole area was bombed in the War and nearly everything was destroyed; the road has gone from one extreme to the other and is now one of the widest parts of the High Street. All day every day wagons used to trundle up and down this street, leaving huge ruts in the road in winter and choking dust in summer. It was a scene of heavy industry as stone was carted from quarry to seafront by men and horses. Arthur Hancock was born in Swanage by the Mill Pond and later entered the family quarrying business. He paints a vivid picture of the comings and goings of the quarrymen's loads:

> 'I remember as a boy, seeing the stone wagons pulling into the railway siding to unload. It was a continual process with the heavy wagons loaded at the quarries pulled by shire horses bringing stone down to the railway yard. Priest's Road was very heavily rutted, and the wagons had a big heavy drag shoe to slow them down the steep hills until they reached the rail yard. Men would be continually loading material to go all over the country. In the quarries in Herston Field you could hear the hammers and chisels chipping away and you could see the horses and donkeys pulling the stone up and every now and again they would lean out of the trace to see how far the cart was coming up. The men looking after the horses would speak to them like human beings and they would respond.'

(Borrett, 2002)

Q What was the purpose of the small metal bars by the front doors of Nos 99-103?

As you go up the street today there are a few interesting buildings. Barley Mow used to be an ale house front room, but had its licence revoked in 1848. Opposite, the temperance movement Figure Head Coffee Tavern, later the Albany Temperance Hotel, was quite popular with some of the townsfolk and visitors but did not attract many quarrymen or working people. The building was severely damaged in an air raid in 1943, as was much of the area, and there is no evidence of it now.

Q What is carved above the door of No. 92?

A little further up is the Congregational Chapel where Wesley preached on his second visit in 1787.

A They are boot scrapers. With all that mud outside, diligent housewives would insist you wipe your boots before coming in off the street.

A A fan – rather ornate for such a small cottage.

Townsend Road on the left before the Black Swan was one of the small lanes that led to the quarries on the hills above Swanage. It now leads up to rough tracks and the Townsend Nature Reserve.

Opposite the pub is a house called The Old Stable, and two stone gate pillars. A few hundred years ago when the Swan was a coaching inn, there must have been a lot of to'ing and fro'ing through these gates.

Further up, at the highest point of the High Street, No. 120 used to be the old Court Hill Post Office up until the early 1970s. To the right of the door stood the post box – notice the filled-in concrete in the pavement here.

Q Can you guess what the terrace of houses on the left are called – the clue is in the stone carving on the end wall?

The old wall fronting the Terrace is attractive with its standing stones. These homes were built in 1893 by Frank Burt (a younger brother of George), as were Gordon Villas (Nos 126—132), a little further down, with their decorative keystone arches.

On the other side of the road, to the right of the barber shop, is Somerley House, once a bakery. During the 19th century the Summers family ran coaches to Wareham from here to meet the train, until shortly after the coming of the railway. Manwell's Lane led up to the meadow where John Wesley preached during his first visit to Swanage in 1774.

205 Parker's is an ancient building and used to be a blacksmiths and later Parker's Stores. Cowlease was the main route to the quarries, mostly lined by quarrymen's cottages, so Parker's was well placed for the quarry traffic. Take this road up the hill.

Q What emblem can you see at the top of this road at Oxford Terrace?

Take the footpath to the right. You are now entering the area known as Townsend, originally a farm of that name covering 162 acres.

Fork left through the mobile homes and keep going straight on up the hill. The quarry workings that used to cover this area are now overlain by mobile homes and above these a peaceful 32-acre nature reserve, looked after by the Dorset Wildlife Trust. Some of the lower quarries were still operating

A cartouche (a stone scroll). Its origin is uncertain, but it is probably 17th century.

A Handfast Terrace. Perhaps the clasped hands have some Masonic link?

until World War II; the higher ones are older and were worked out long before. David Haysom remembers the area before it was developed – when the whole hill was an open 'playground' when he was growing up. Then in the mid-1970s mobile homes were installed on top of the old workings, the land not being stable enough for anything else.

Stick to the footpath going uphill to the nature reserve (there are no signs to guide you). As you enter the reserve an old quarry entrance has been fenced off. Note: you cannot go down the mine for safety reasons and because of disturbing the inmates.

Q What likes to 'hang out' in old underground quarries and why?

Imagine this area in its working day. A donkey is harnessed to a long pole or spack. It trudges round the capstan in the centre, winding the chain attached to the quarr cart underground, on which sits a great slab of rough stone. Slowly the stone is brought to the surface. More or less open sheds encircle the quarry, allowing the men to cut and dress the stone on site, in all weathers. Waste stone is piled up in spoil heaps all round the area (now grassed over), dug out from quarry holes. 'Lanes' or tunnels run in all directions to reach the beds of stone, and the sound of men at work with hammer and chisel echoes round the hill.

Townsend Nature Reserve is an area of banks of waste stone or 'scars' and subsidence. For part of the year horses graze the turf, keeping it short and scrub-free.

A Bats love the stable temperature and humidity of caves. The old tunnels or 'lanes' are now home to several species, including the rare Greater Horseshoe Bat.

Q The two broken stones in the centre braced the capstan. Why do you think they were called 'crab stones'?

At Durlston an old quarry working has been preserved.

Take the path to the left and explore. Much of the reserve is SSSI (a Site of Special Scientific Interest). Seven species of orchids have been recorded here and the unimproved grassland and chalk-loving flowers attract butterflies – Small Blue (larvae feed on Kidney Vetch), Meadow Brown and Marbled White (both feeding on grass), Field Grasshoppers and Bush Crickets. Buddleia, which is favoured by some butterflies, has colonised the disturbed ground.

Q Can you guess what wild mammals live here?

Q What do you think created the small mounds in the grassland?

Feel free to follow any of the tracks, some of which link to Durlston Country Park. If you keep going parallel to the town following the yellow footpath signs you'll come to a gate. The lane to the right leads to Anvil Point Lighthouse. Instead turn left towards town. On the left behind the railings is a mock-up of a quarry entrance, part of the Townsend Centre, a field studies

A Yellow meadow ants. If you're lucky, you may see a green woodpecker feeding on them.

A Roe deer, foxes, badgers and plenty of rabbits.

A They were originally shaped like the pincers of a crab and held the capstan in place.

This slab of stone with its dinosaur footprint was discovered by local builder John F. Wright while digging the foundations of Sunshine House.

resource. On the distant hill in front are two large buildings: Harrow House International College and Purbeck View School for special needs children, which used to be a private school. Swanage at one time was full of private schools for children of the well-to-do.

Q What is set in the wall by the front steps of Sunshine House?

Opposite at No. 21, in 1981 Dave Selby was constructing a garage. During excavations 170 footprints thought to be *Megalosaurus* and *Iguanodon* (three-toed dinosaurs which walked on their hind legs) were found. Most of the slabs were taken up and have been preserved in the Dorset County Museum; you might just be able to make out some footprints in the large weathered slab on the side of the drive.

Halfway down the road, turn right into Queens Road. Mount Scar on the right is an old council-run school. The Congregational Cemetery is on your left. Carry straight on to the corner and Clarence Cottage. A bomb fell in the garden here during World War II, bounced off the wall and exploded horizontally lower down the hill, as a result causing more damage than if it had fallen vertically.

Go round the corner to the right, then at No. 51 take the alley back on yourself to the left and go straight down the hill back to the High Street.

A A fossilised ammonite and a stone slab with a dinosaur footprint.

Walk 6:
Station Road and Along the Prom

Start and finish: Swanage Railway Station
Approx. distance: 2.5 km
Terrain: Pavement, beach and promenade, level

As Station Road led straight from the railway station to the beach, it evolved into the main road for shops and entertainment. On the left look for the three buildings used at different times as cinemas. The Mowlem near the beach is now the only cinema in town.

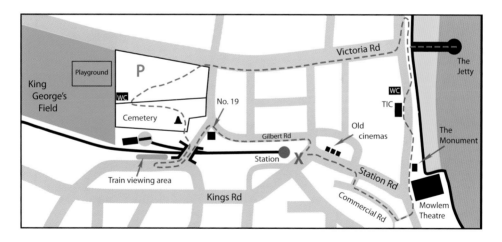

As you enter Commercial Road there is a rather ornate Victorian downpipe, and up on the wall a bust of Shakespeare (for no particular reason other than Burt liked to adorn Swanage with cultural pieces). The name Commercial Road is rather a misnomer, as this area was originally not used by commercial retailers but instead served as storage yards for stone and coal. A rail track ran through to the station and there used to be a sign outside The Old Stable stating: 'To prevent accidents goods must not be left on or by the sides of tramway, 1893'. Most of this disappeared in 1906, the lines were taken up and the buildings became workshops and stores. Only now is the area true to its original commercial name, with many small businesses and offices.

Take the alley towards the sea front. For more than a century, the old Mowlem Institute fulfilled its original purpose: '...for the benefit and mutual improvement of the working classes' and for 'occasional meetings on freemasonry'. Today its replacement, the Mowlem Theatre, is described tactfully as 'an imposing building' housing a cinema, theatre, restaurant and small arcade of shops and acting as a community centre.

Along the seafront pay your respects to John Mowlem at the Alfred the Great Monument. This rather bizarre memorial commemorates a battle involving Viking ships, though it is unlikely any battle took place, and certainly not here. Instead it is more likely the boats were wrecked on Peveril Ledges. Neither did Alfred have cannon balls. The ones atop the column are Russian from the Crimean War, brought to Britain embedded in the hulls of wooden warships returning from the War.

Years ago on Swanage's beach you could not change openly without risk of offending someone; instead, you either erected your own tent for 15 old pence a week or hired one of the statics for 3 old pence (men) or 4 old pence (ladies) a day. Norah Kaye lived nearly all her life in Swanage and remarked: 'Even at the end of the thirties there were still bathing machines in Swanage, we were a bit behind the times here' (Borrett, 2002).

Head towards the Tourist Information Centre, known locally as the White House.

Q If you 'throw a coin and hit the bell you may have good luck as well' – where can you find this inscription?

The building was taken over as the Air Raid Precautions Headquarters and later became the Home Guard HQ early in World War II. Along with all the south coast, Swanage was declared a Designated Defence and Prohibited Area. The White House was walled with sandbags, the cliff-tops barb wired, the beach out of bounds – displaying steel scaffolding along the whole bay area into the water, concrete dragons' teeth along the promenade and more barbed wire on the sand to stop enemy landings – quite a different picture to today.

Further along the promenade, the cliff-top buildings are precariously perched atop the soft Wealden Beds. These attractive orange-red, unconsolidated mudstones and sands are basically eroded bits of Dartmoor

Wartime beach defences. (From the David Haysom collection.)

washed down here in Wealden times (Cretaceous period) by fast-flowing rivers. The Beds are exceptionally thick (up to 600 m) at Swanage and run all the way, gradually thinning, to Worbarrow Bay 17 km away.

Swanage Bay, with the chalk headlands standing out to the north, hard limestone cliffs to the south and soft Wealden Beds in between, is what is known as a discordant coast. Here man battles the sea and it's not certain who's winning. The concrete prom and buildings along the shore stop the Wealden cliffs eroding into the sea, but then the beaches become depleted of sand as the cliffs no longer erode. Construction in 1993 of the Jetty (sometimes called Banjo Quay because of its shape) to divert flood waters away from Station Road and out to the centre of the Bay may not have helped as it interrupted the natural movement of sand. The groynes can't stop the sand going out but they do slow the movement from one end of the beach to the other. Beach replenishment work is an ongoing task and it was last carried out in 2005/6, using sand dredged from Poole Harbour. DEFRA estimates it will need redoing every 10 years or so, though with rising sea levels it could be sooner.

The oldest part of the promenade dates back to the late 1800s (near the eastern end); the rest of the wall was built around 1903/5. The Bay geology is complex and changes over short distances, making the cliffs here rather unstable, as do the springs, which result in gullying and mud flows. The *Swanage Times* (17 February 1977) reported: 'the cliffs at the north end of the bay … have for some years been subject to falls … a few years ago a greenhouse and conservatory crashed down the cliffs from gardens above'. Pebbles collect here and in places ridge up to form a semi-permanent storm beach, which protects the base of the cliffs from wave action. During calm weather the beach builds up, so that visitors in autumn will see a different picture to visitors in spring.

The Jetty. (Photographer Simon Twilley.)

Cliff falls are not unusual in Swanage Bay and heavy rainfall in winter 2012/13 produced dangerous landslides towards the north end of the beach. A number of beach huts were buried and the promenade became impassable in places. Swanage now has its own Coastal Change Forum, affiliated to the Dorset Coast Forum (see above), which helps local people understand the processes that lie behind coastal erosion and assists in coordination of the clear-up after an event.

'There's a guy who's been doing the deckchairs and boats forever', according to local, Dave Tompkins. He is referring to Barry Wiggins.

> *'I was born in Swanage and have always done it. In the morning I set out the deckchairs, put the pedalos down at the water's edge, get the canoes out and put up the signposts. It used to be a living, but not now...now I just keep it going. My two sons help in summer. We have a couple o' hundred chairs, it used to be a few thousand. Nowadays people bring everything with them. In the old days, the coaches would pull up, there used to be a mad dash to the beach, they'd grab the chairs and form a circle. They'd put newspaper on their heads if it rained. Holidaymakers would come on the train for 2 weeks and stay here, regardless of the weather. Now they come and go by car – if the weather's bad, they leave. We don't have the hotels we used to – the big hotels that held a lot of people have all been knocked down. If it wasn't for the elderly people coming in on the coaches for the*

day, we wouldn't keep going. The old people like to sit in a chair on the wall. It's part of the enjoyment of being there.

We've been fairly trouble-free – haven't had any incidents with the boats, etc. Someone died in a deckchair once, one of the collectors went round and found him. You don't want too many of those! We have a rescue boat and someone on hand for the pedalos, but with Health and Safety we're not supposed to touch anyone. If someone sees somebody in trouble they're supposed to go to the Information Point. But in 15 minutes a rubber dinghy can blow a long way out to sea. We have a good system going, not technically right, but you've got to be practical.'

Swanage beach. (Photographer Simon Twilley.)

Wander as far as you like along the beach, but then you'll need to turn back to Victoria Avenue. At King George's Field (behind the large car park) children and dogs can let off steam on the playing fields and in the play area.

In the cemetery on the hill to the left are some beautiful headstones. Under a pyramid-shaped pile of Guernsey stone lies John Mowlem and his wife.

Q What was the name of John Mowlem's wife and at what age did she die?

A Susannah, aged 61.

The Mowlem Vault (in the middle distance) was built by John Mowlem himself of Guernsey stone, testament to the importance of the Guernsey quarries to his firm's fortunes.

Leave through the gate by Mowlem's Vault. Stand on the bridge to view the railway engine shed, turntable and other action on the line or pop along to the viewing area the other side of the bridge. Then double back to Gilbert Road and the Railway Station.

Q What is the name of the patient dog in the window at No. 19 Gilbert Road?

Q What animal is painted on the coaches and engines of the Swanage Railway?

A A lion, the standardised logo of British Railways.

A Donut.

Other Walks and Cycling Routes

Discover Old Swanage

Every Tuesday and Wednesday, from Easter to the end of September, two local historians – David Haysom (Honorary Curator of the Swanage Museum and Heritage Centre) and Stewart Borrett – lead visitors on a fascinating guided circular town walk. Meet outside the Heritage Centre in the Square at 2.30 p.m. Duration 1–2 hours. Free of charge, but donations to the Centre are welcome.

Walking and Cycling Trails

Leaflets on Swanage walking trails:
- Town Trail (less than 1 mile);
- Stone Trail (1 mile);
- Victorian Trail (2 miles).

(Available from the Swanage Museum and Heritage Centre and TIC.)

The websites www.virtual-swanage.co.uk and www.dorsetforyou. com/396552 have suggestions for local bike rides, and the Pedal Around Purbeck map shows how all the routes interlink.

Purbeck Freewheelers organise guided rides around Purbeck April to August, starting at Purbeck Sports Centre in Wareham (tel. 01929 554550).

The South West Coast Path
(www.nationaltrail.co.uk)

The South West Coast Path is the longest national trail in England, starting at Poole Harbour and covering 630 miles. It skirts along Ballard Down, then dips down to the town, along the Bay and out to Peveril Point, then continuing on round Durlston Bay and westwards. Just keep the sea on one side and follow the acorn waymarks.

Ballard Down

The chalk ridge of Ballard Down was caused by a huge fold in the rocks; a band of hard limestone forms the headland, softer clays the eroded bays either side. At one time this ridge was joined to the Needles on the Isle of Wight. If you walk eastwards along the centuries-old highway atop the Down (now the Purbeck Way), you may 'Rest and be thankful' at the stone further along the ridge. Smugglers often used this ridgeway, with the witch Jinny Gould's cottage a useful half-way house for storing contraband on their way westwards. Bill Bryson described the stunning view from here in *Notes from a Small Island*:

'*For miles around the Dorset Hills rolled and billowed, like a shaken-out blanket settling onto a bed. ... It was beautiful beyond words, one of those rare moments when life seems perfect.*'

View of Swanage Bay (© iStockphoto.com/Sanna Wicks).

Ballard Down is owned by the National Trust and is a Site of Special Scientific Interest, important for wildflowers and butterflies, including rare Adonis Blues, which appear in spring with a second brood in late summer, and Chalkhill Blues, which emerge in July. Volunteers are helping to tackle the pervasive spread of gorse, and livestock keep the sward (turf) short. As elsewhere, the different farmers and landowners can be a challenge for conservationists.

On the hill above Ulwell you cannot miss the Obelisk, a prominent landmark – perhaps too prominent as the first obelisk was supposedly taken down in 1941 to prevent it being a landmark for invading Germans. The Royal Engineers re-erected it in 1973 and it is a rewarding climb to the top to enjoy fine views of the county for miles around. The Obelisk sits on a prehistoric round barrow. This was excavated in the mid-19th century and a grave pit 14 ft below the surface was found to contain a skeleton, which appeared to have been trussed up before burial, perhaps to prevent spirit walking. The original obelisk installed on top of the mound by Burt collapsed shortly afterwards, was re-erected, then later fell down again (or was taken down by the military, it is not sure which); superstition holds that it was the dead man trying to free himself from his bondage that caused the obelisk to collapse.

(Photographer David Leadbetter, from the book Paranormal Purbeck.*)*

Another mile on along Ballard Down you come to Handfast Point and Old Harry Rocks. The distinctive chalk and flint pillars are sadly being eroded away by the sea at their base. Whether you are looking at Old Harry himself or his Wife is the source of local contention. Some claim Old Harry's Wife succumbed to the sea the night of the big storm (1896) which also claimed the lifeboat from Swanage. Others reckon it was the Old Man himself who gave way to his more stalwart (and still-standing) wife. These rocks have seen many shipwrecks off their point. They are said to be 80 million years old. See the chapter on folklore.

Priest's Way

In days gone by the priest from Worth Matravers would trek from Worth to minister in the much smaller fishing village of Swanage, 4 miles away. By 1506 the town warranted its own parish church and vicar, yet Priest's Way continued to be used by locals. It cuts through the heart of the old quarries, sheltered by stone walls on either side and meandering across open fields, with fine views on the way. The added advantage is that The Square and Compass pub at Worth acts as a halfway house.

Priest's Way. (Picture supplied by Virtual Swanage (www.virtualswanage.co.uk), photographer Andrew Dorey.)

Help and Information

Tourist Information Centre (TIC),
The White House, Shore Road

Tel. 01929 422885, email: mail@swanage.gov.uk,
www.visitswanageandpurbeck.co.uk
www.swanage.gov.uk

Open Monday to Saturday 10 a.m. to 5 p.m. all year and also Sundays during summer.

There is a first-aid point here. A board outside gives details of the tides, boating byelaws and other council notices.

Swanage Museum and Heritage Centre, The Square

Tel. 01929 421427 (Museum), 01929 423850 (Local Studies)
email: swanagemuseum@swanagemuseum.plus.com,
www.swanagemuseum.co.uk

Open daily from Easter to October, then weekends till New Year. Free entry.

The Centre has several recreated scenes featuring life in the town, together with display panels that tell the story of Swanage from dinosaurs to World War II. The interactive displays are great for children, and local historians are often on hand to answer any local and family history questions. The Museum arranges talks throughout the year, as well as historical guided walks around town during the summer months, led by the Honorary Curator, David Haysom, and local historian, Stewart Borrett.

The Museum has a separate Local Studies Room at Marine Villas on the Pier. Viewing is strictly by appointment (donations welcome). This facility has a wide range of original and facsimile material for local and family history research, including old photographs, maps, copies of Parish Registers dating back to 1563, trade directories, and old local newspapers on microfilm from the mid 1800s through to the 1930s. Anyone interested in carrying out research or becoming a researcher should contact the Swanage Museum.

Swanage Library, High Street

Tel. 01929 423485, email: swanagelibrary@dorsetcc.gov.uk,
www.dorsetforyou.com/libraries
Closed Tuesdays, Thursdays and Sundays.

The library offers:
- free internet access for 30 minutes, then £1 for every half-hour thereafter; children can use the computers free for up to 2 hours a day;
- a session for young people on Monday evenings (5–6.30 p.m.), library-based activities and games planned with staff and the children, term time only;
- story time for toddlers every Friday from 11–11.30 a.m;
- school holiday activities, a reading challenge in the summer and class visits;
- Chatterbooks reading and activities session on Saturday afternoon, the second Saturday in the month, to encourage boys and girls to read, term time only;
- a drop-in for TREATS (The Resources Equipment and Toy Store), allowing you to borrow toys;
- adult career advice sessions, Tuesday afternoons, by appointment only;
- a resource for Purbeck Special Needs School;
- reading groups (there are about 13 different groups in Swanage);
- a home library service, with deliveries to house-bound people and people in care homes, run by RVS volunteers as part of the outreach programme;
- drop-in Adult Discussion Group, last Wednesday in the month, led by staff member.

The Beach and Beach Bungalows

Tel. the TIC on 01929 422885 or 0870 4420680, email: mail@swanage.gov.uk,
http://www.swanage.gov.uk/beachhuts/beachbungalows.pdf

Swanage beach has won awards and been awarded Blue Flag status. Each summer a small protected bathing zone is cordoned off to restrict watercraft and allow for safe bathing, and between 1 May and 30 September Shore Road is closed to general traffic between Station Road and Victoria Avenue; alas the beach is also closed to dogs during this period to comply with its Blue Flag status.

Council beach huts (nos 1–32) along Shore Road are available for hire. The access path is between nos 26 and 27 and the toilets are situated next to no. 1 (which may or may not be a bonus to you). Tap water and waste bins can be found near both the toilets and access path. You can also hire bungalows at The Spa (between Shore Road and De Moulham Road). Toilets are situated behind no. 12, roughly in the middle of the campus. Dogs are allowed in these bungalows and all are day-use only (no overnight stays permitted). Fees range considerably, from £22 per week at Easter and after the summer holidays to a peak of £144 during summer. Hire includes four chairs, a fold-down table and electric power point. During winter the huts on the beach have to be taken up because of strong east winds.

Swanage beach. Signs at the eastern end of the prom say private, but the public is allowed to use the beach here and you can walk all the way to the chalk cliff (© iStockphoto.com/Sanna Wicks).

Maps

The general area is covered by OS map OL15 Purbeck and South Dorset. A detailed map of the town is available free from the TIC.

References and Further Reading

Ashley H (1992) *The Dorset Coast: History, Lore and Legend.* Countryside Books, Newbury.

Benfield E (2011) *Purbeck Shop: A Stoneworker's Story of Stone.* Cambridge University Press, Cambridge.

Borrett S (2002) *Swanage in the 1920s and 1930s.* Amberwood Graphics, Wareham.

Borrett S (2010) *Swanage in World War II.* Amberwood Graphics, Wareham.

Borrett S (2012) *Swanage Wartime Childhood.* Amberwood Graphics, Wareham.

Briggs K (1991) *A Dictionary of British Folk-tales in the English Language.* Routledge, London.

Canning AD, Maxted KR (1983) *Coastal Studies in Purbeck.* Purbeck Press, Swanage.

Chaffey J (2006) *Purbeck Landscapes.* Dorset Books, Tiverton.

Cooper I (2008) *Purbeck Revealed.* James Pembroke Publishing/Ilay Cooper, Langton.

Hardy WM (1906) *Smuggling Days in Purbeck.* Purbeck Press, Swanage.

Hardy WM (1908) *Old Swanage.* Dorset County Chronicle Printing Works, Dorchester.

Glaister M, Oxley P (2012) *Dorset.* Rockfax, Sheffield.

Haysom D (2010) *Discover Old Swanage.* Roving Press, Frampton.

Haysom D, Bragg D (1991) *Swanage and Purbeck in Old Photographs.* Sutton, Stroud.

Haysom D, Patrick J (1992) *Swanage in Old Picture Postcards.* European Library, Zaltbommel.

Hyland P (1989) *Purbeck: The Ingrained Island.* Dovecote Press, Wimborne.

Hyland P (1998) *Isle of Purbeck.* Dovecote Press, Wimborne.

Leadbetter D (2013) *Paranormal Purbeck: A Study of the Unexplained.* Roving Press, Frampton.

Lewer D (1986) *The Story of Swanage. A History From Early Times.* Harewood, Bournemouth.

Lewer D (1990) *John Mowlem's Swanage.* Dorset Publishing Co., Wincanton.

Lewer D, Calkin JB (2007) *Curiosities of Swanage. Or Old London by the Sea.* Purbeck Press, Swanage.

Lewer D, Smale D (1994, 2004) *Swanage Past.* Phillimore, Chichester.

Mitchell V, Smith K (1986) *Branch Line to Swanage.* Middleton Press, Midhurst.

Mitchell V, Smith K (2003) *Wareham to Swanage: 50 Years of Change.* Middleton Press, Midhurst.

Norman A (2005) *Enid Blyton and Her Enchantment with Dorset.* Halsgrove, Tiverton.

Stanier P (1998) *The Industrial Past.* Dovecote Press, Wimborne.

Thomas J (1998) *Stone Quarrying.* Dovecote Press, Wimborne.

Tringham S (1976) *The Bollard Story: How London's Street Posts Came to Swanage.* Available at Durlston Visitor Centre.

Warren D (2004) *Curious Dorset.* Sutton, Stroud.

Wessex Archaeology (2004) *Archaeological Desk-based Assessment and Walkover Survey.* Report 56580.02. Available at Durlston Visitor Centre.

Other Roving Press Titles

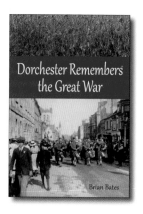

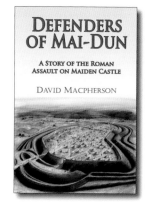

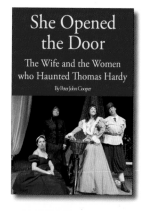

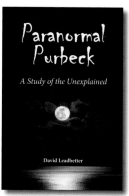

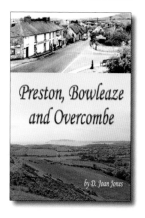

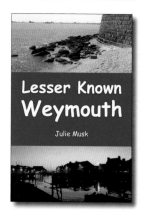

If you like exploring, you'll love our books

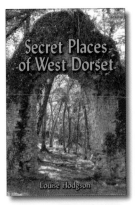

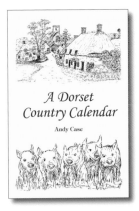

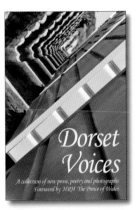

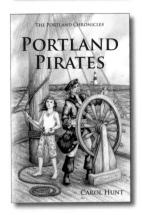

Roving
Press

www.rovingpress.co.uk

Index